Principles
of
gestalt
family therapy

Principles
of
gestalt
family therapy

A GESTALT-EXPERIENTIAL HANDBOOK

by

Walter Kempler, M. D.

First Printing, Norway, 1973
Second Printing, Norway, 1974
Third Printing, U.S.A., 1974
Fourth Printing, U.S.A., 1978

Cover picture: The Dawn of Awareness

Script: Grace Greenwald

Published and distributed through
THE KEMPLER INSTITUTE
Costa Mesa, California
Postbox 1692
U.S.A. 92626

Printed in the United States of America
Library of Congress Catalog Number:
74-26006
International Standard Book Number:
0-9600808-1-3

Deseret Press
Salt Lake City, Utah

To Mindy who gave me the strength,
And Abe, the courage to use it.
To Fritz who quickened my way,
And Marlynn who stirs me to lose it.

Contents

Introduction

Some years ago, while walking along a busy shipping pier with my young son, Adam, and amiably chatting about the various wharf activities, he made a remark about the hydraulic loading operations which I considered uncanny wisdom for his five brief years on this earth. I shared my amazement with him and he replied quite casually, "Oh, I know everything. Only sometimes I need to be reminded."

Adam, in his innocence, not only expounded the ancient Hindu belief that all knowledge lies locked within each of us waiting to be "reminded" into consciousness, but he also "reminded" me of the purpose of family.

Similarly, when parents squabble and a child takes a side, the child needs to be reminded to butt out. And, should the parents consistently hide their struggling in belated, nocturnal bedroom battles, the family therapist needs to remind them of the advantages of immediate responsiveness and of the benefits children get from witnessing the sometimes necessarily anguished negotiations of intimate living.

A family may be likened to an archipelago: to a cluster of islands surrounded by the common waters of time flowing faithfully towards the sea of eternity. The various shapes of these juxtaposed islands create unique currents: currents which, in turn, influence the contours—the personalities—of each.

It is these influential, invisible currents which call the attention of the family therapist; and, it is his task to "remind" the islands about them, to show them the adverse currents which are responsible for the painful and unnecessary erosion of persons within this archipelagian family.

A family conversation is the therapist's device for making visible those various currents. As family members talk together, no matter the topic, both the beneficial as well as the corroding influences will become evident.

Using the strength that lies restlessly within each of them, the therapist will "remind" them of forgotten desires which he will then guide to their proper destination. Storms of desire and protest will characterize the therapeutic scene, leaving in its wake, new perspectives and refreshing behavior. And, if the therapist is truly successful he, too, will be changed.

Family Diagnoses

There can be no adequate terminology for labelling families. Not because there are so many factors at play, although that would be reason enough, but because one does not in fact talk about the families at all when describing them. One talks only about one's own perspective; how he sees what's happening according to his own conceptualization of happenings.

Terms like sibling rivalry are useless: they do not point. Parents come in and say, "There's too much friction among our kids." The therapist's label of Sibling Rivalry only restates the parental remark. There is nothing that indicates when kids fight excessively there is parental abdication. Parental abdication might be a better "diagnosis" but it, too, though it points to the target, says little.

Likewise, terms like double bind and scapegoating are useless and distracting. Such patterns can be found in any family. Double binding is an inherent aspect of all relating, not of certain families. It reflects the underlying paradoxical desire to be both with and apart, to join and to separate, that is everyone's lot. Some manage it better than others. It is pointless to talk about it. The same goes for scapegoating. It serves no purpose to characterize a relationship as scapegoated. The oldest child of an immigrant family who learns the new language first, becomes the appreciated family spokesman, and later becomes a contented and successful linguist could be said to have been scapegoated. The dynamic is the same. To what end does it serve to use such terms?

A diagnostic label or description to be of value must point the way; must, by the awareness it provides, move us outward from the difficulty and not into it or onto it so that we can nod knowingly at one another with a satisfying, "Yup! Another case of scapegoating."

Diagnoses are the tombstones of the therapist's frustration, and accusations such as, defensive, resistant and secondary gain, are the flowers placed on the grave of his buried dissatisfaction. No one scapegoats, no one is defensive, no one wants his self-defeating behavior. Everyone who comes to therapy, including the reluctant family member, is motivated. The only issue is the therapist's ability to influence. If there is to be a diagnosis, there is only one: Therapist Incompetence.

As the therapist's skills improve and his perspective changes, his behavior becomes more effective. An "impossible" type parent this year will be seen next year as a sound parent in need of some simple but forceful guidance: the therapist has improved. A difficult type of family this year may become an exciting family next year: the therapist's skills are increasing.

There need be no shame about incompetence. Its recognition begins a struggle which, if successful, is never completely won. Nor need there be any guilt for the many years that the rap has been laid on the patient with name calling fancifully entitled, "The Diagnosis"; and ill-advised allegations like "defensive" and "resistant." Once the therapist's frustration about his own limitations is recognized and shared, diagnoses disappear. And gradually, so will his incompetence.

Discoverers start with specific personal experiences, find generalities which they discard upon the world and return their attention to what's in front of them. Because of its inherent merit, the discarded (published) generality is grasped by the hapless and used to

11

make themselves blind. Much uncreative time is enjoyably wasted seeing how far the generality will go. The so-called adolescent emancipation years, for instance, are measured more than they are questioned.

The correct path is the discoverer's path—from the specific to the general. This volume does not concern itself with the generalities of family life. It directs the reader to look for his own specifics before him, to become his own discoverer. It urges him to see for himself whether the adolescent before him is searching for emancipation, identification, retrenchment, or whatever the therapist may choose to call what happens between them; and to ignore the preconceived notions of others.

Additionally, it suggests that he see the happening as a composite of himself and the other, and to know that he and whoever he faces at that moment create whatever phenomenon he may choose to describe. Thus, concepts like the adolescent emancipation years will be replaced by a specific, personal, inimitable discovery, such as, "Paul's mother is frantic about Paul's struggle for new separateness within his family. It's hard for her to know just where to draw the line, when to give Paul his own head and when to stop him. I wish Father would help them more instead of only begging for peace and quiet around the house. I trust Paul and think he goes further than he himself desires in order to arouse some guiding interest from his father. So, at this moment, there is Mother's worry, Father's disinterest, Paul's challenge and my (the therapist's) belief that Mother should turn to Father for help instead of fighting with Paul; and we are all struggling together to find some solution that will satisfy each of us. I wonder if Mother realizes what a fine job she has done with Paul. I must remember to tell her next time. Maybe it will relieve her anxiety a bit."

Such "Diagnoses" may lack the glamour of the succinct phrase, but by ploughing our specific thoughts promptly back into our work instead of trying to generalize them out, work can become more exciting, the fruits of our labor more gratifying and the risk of blinding our colleagues less likely.

GESTALT vs. GESTALT-EXPERIENTIAL vs. EXPERIENTIAL

When Fritz Perls and I first met, he was toying with the thought of calling his work Gestalt Therapy while I called my work simply Family Therapy. We had much in common and for a brief time we worked together. We both believed, for instance, history taking was useless and analysis distracting. We saw the existential encounter—the face to face meeting in the immediate moment—as the essential force in the therapeutic process. Although in agreement theoretically, we split over the issue of the therapist's personal participation. Fritz found it more comfortable to work with the hot-seat model which placed him outside of the immediate encounter, while I tenaciously opposed any therapist—including Fritz—hiding behind any device whatsoever.

Not that devices and gimmicks are bad per se. They can be most useful. It is the hiding I oppose. Since gimmicks can so easily shield the therapist from uncomfortable exposure and fantasied vulnerability, and since I believe the richness of the therapeutic experience is directly dependent upon the reciprocity in the encounter (though, not only that), the gimmick represents, from the therapist's side, the greatest hazard to the therapeutic process.

For awhile, I called my professional activities Gestalt Family Therapy. When Fritz and I parted professionally—we never parted in spirit—I bandied between the titles of Experiential and Gestalt-Experiential. I felt a continued kinship with Fritz, but also a need to emphasize the mutuality in the experience between patient and therapist. Now I believe that this difference between me and Fritz is less, if indeed, it exists at all. In his last years, Fritz recognized and warned against the coming of the Gestalt Gimmicist. Also, since we split, the mystery for me of the strange marriage between his effectiveness and his gimmickry has been solved. Fritz knew that he filled in with gimmicks. He used them, but he suffered them. Fritz was a profoundly honest man.

Unfortunately, for Fritz and for those who loved him, Fritz could only suffer alone—in private. A serious problem today in the Gestalt movement is a consequence of that fact. Many of his admirers, having seen and personally experienced the success of the gimmicks without sharing the suffering of the man, simply try to copy what they tasted.

Fritz was a specialist. His genius rested in his ability to maintain his separateness, and revealed itself in the skillfulness with which he helped others to gain their needed separateness. But when it came to union—the other side of the spinning coin of life—he either opposed it or was helpless. Consequently, he attracted mostly those who struggled for separateness and those who needed comfort in their stuck separateness. As a result, the Gestalt movement is temporarily out of balance with too much emphasis on "I am I" and not nearly enough appreciation for the equally necessary and difficult struggle for union. Although the best preparation for union is the successful separation, it is not enough for the therapist to stop his work at that point. Neither separateness nor union is the goal of the therapeutic process, but rather the exhortation of the endless and often painful undulation between them.

Once the hot-seat model, along with all the now familiar tactics and terms (e.g., What are you trying to do to me now?) are recognized as the hard won tactics of the professional Fritz, and the emphasis on separateness appreciated as part of the karma of the personal Fritz, then the movement which crystallized about his life can continue the task of finding better (therapeutic, if you prefer) ways to meet each other in the creative style of his life—experientially—rather than by copying his particular style of working. For me then, there is no difference between Gestalt, Gestalt-Experiential and Experiential.

One may ask, "How, then, is it possible to identify a Gestalt therapist?" Hopefully, it will not be too obvious. Certainly not by the popularity of the tactics he uses, but perhaps by their uniqueness and the authenticity with which they are lived.

My life begins with Us.

When We cease, I discover You-and-Me.
Sometimes I long for Us: sometimes I prefer You-and-Me.
Sometimes neither suffices and I fill with desire.

Then, there are things I can learn to do:

I can learn to speak the more I want.
I can learn to say "No!" when I don't want.
I can learn how best to insist, and when to look elsewhere.

And when desire must be revised, I can grieve.

Without You I cannot learn.
Somehow, I must learn through You, with You.
Alone, I can only ache and scream.

In your need You come.

And, when we touch
I somehow learn to do
Some of what I can learn to do.

And, You, I call my family.

Family is the imperative You: the essential other. Family is a kind of relatedness, roughly approximating the family in which one lives.
To restore or to develop the visible family as the collective, indigenous You for each of its members, is the task of the Gestalt family therapist.

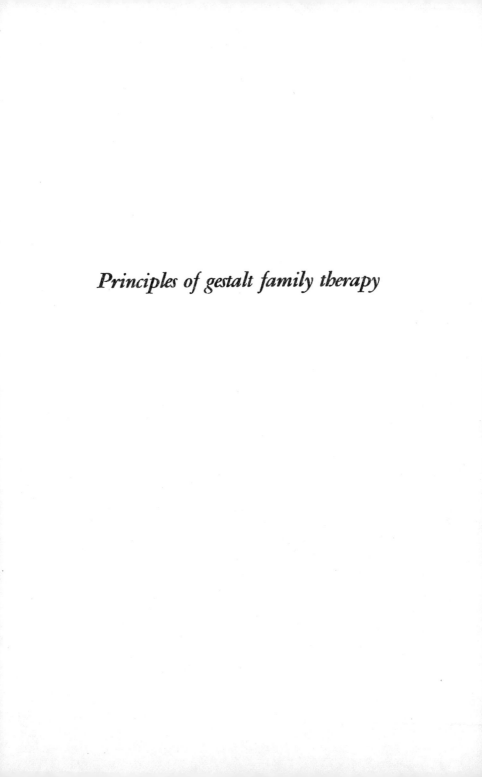

Principles of gestalt family therapy

Basic information for the Newcomer

Gestalt Family Therapy is a model for the treatment of the troubled individual in the context of family. Its central premise assumes that a symptomatic individual, regardless of the nature of the symptom—physical, psychological or interpersonal—is simply saying, "Ouch! I have a pain in my family."

This approach is predicated on the notion that through the proper kind of union between people, necessary separateness and differentiation occur which, in turn, serves the cause of further union; and that, when this undulating process is flowing, family members do not become persistently symptomatic.

The goal of Gestalt Family Therapy is to restore the family to its proper function as the chief resource for the personal needs of its members, adults and children, alike.

The therapist's equipment consists of common sense, some skill at guiding intimate conversation, and a willingness to participate personally.

1. INDICATIONS FOR FAMILY THERAPY

Family therapy is recommended for any paired adult in distress regardless of the nature of the symptom. Couples exert a vital and reciprocal influence on one another's behavior. That influence belongs in the treatment.

I have headaches.

My husband and I quarrel constantly.

I'm nervous all the time.

Ever since my mother died, I've been depressed.

My mother-in-law is destroying our marriage.

The premise holds though the symptom antedates the relationship and seems uniquely singular.

I've been overweight since my teens.

I can't stop gambling (drinking, smoking, etc.).

I am bi-sexual, and it causes me much difficulty. My wife doesn't know, and I wouldn't want her to find out. Our relationship is fine. (Absurd!)

And it includes current difficulties seemingly outside the family.

My probation officer sent me.

My patients drive me crazy.

2. WHEN TO INCLUDE CHILDREN

When a child is symptomatic or is associated with the announced problem, then both parents and all the children living at home are seen together.

Perry, our eight year old, is still wetting the bed.

We have a retarded daughter.

I'm afraid that I will harm one of my children.

Our 15 year old ran away from home last week.

Linda is having trouble at school and the school counselor suggested therapy.

There is no such thing as a problem limited to one child. Noxious family influences, though unevenly distributed, touch everyone. Furthermore, every family forms a mosaic in which all members are relatively situated. A family with one "bad" child, for instance, invariably will have a "good" child whose behavior, though less annoying, is also self-defeating.

3. WHEN TO DISMISS CHILDREN FROM THE THERAPY

When parents are struggling successfully to create a mutually satisfying relationship between them, the atmosphere in the family is nutritious for children and children do not become persistently disturbed. To consider an extreme example, a retarded child need not be a disturbed child. A retarded child may be an unusually disturbing presence in the family, but when the parents are well joined, help is sought when needed and adjustments are made where necessary.

Note: Parents need not be successful, they need only be struggling successfully; which means that they are neither deadlocked in a cold truce, nor settled into unrewarding compromises which shadow or use the children.

Since the healthy struggling between parents in search of a mutually satisfying relationship is seen as the most influential activity in the family, it remains the target center for all therapeutic effort —not to the exclusion of all else, but as the constant reference point for all work.

Symptomatic children then are considered pawns caught in the web of parental incompatibility. As soon as they can be dis-

21

entangled, and there is sufficient evidence that they can be kept out of the parental conflict, children may be dismissed from the treatment. (Subsequent participation is permitted on request, or, when a serious topic is met in the therapy that directly concerns one of them.)

Children either remain or are dismissed from the treatment as a single unit. Exception: a pre-verbal child may be exempted when not identified as part of the problem and its behavior is distracting. Unique circumstances may require further modification of this proposition, such as a child away at school, an uninvolved teenager preparing to move from the parental home, or serious parental objection. But as a rule, this latter should be opposed.

Exception:
When parents come for simple guidance in the management of a problem with a child whose behavior is disturbing to them, and their goal remains undaunted by the therapist's orientation, all the children remain in the treatment throughout its limited course.

4. THE PRIVATE SESSION

Avoid individual interviews whenever possible. It can arouse unnecessary jealousies, needless suspicions, and it puts the therapist in the role of a confidant with secrets. Instead, a family discussion concerning the request is advised. Such a conversation can be of value to all, including the requistioner; even more than a secret revelation to the therapist.

If, however, an urgent request for a private session is granted, the therapist is ever alert for the remarks which require privacy. Even the most casual comment such as,

> It seems so relaxed here without the family

is best met with,

> Is that something you couldn't say in front of your spouse?

An honest fear of disaster usually motivates the request for privacy. The family member fears hurting or being hurt by the disclosure. Often, a confession of infidelity is the carefully guarded secret. In such instances it is necessary to clarify the difference between appropriate privacy and destructive secrecy. There is only one potentially damaging secret in intimate relating: withholding feelings, thoughts or attitudes toward the other. All else is private and sharing is optional. In circumstances as above, a discussion with the spouse about what is missing in their relationship is more to the point than telling the therapist (or the spouse for that matter) what is provided elsewhere.

Anything said that pertains to a family member is directed back to the next family session and its disclosure is left to the discretion of the privateer.

> *Wife:* There are many things I cannot discuss with my husband.
>
> *Therapist:* I suggest that you discuss that with him next session.

5. THE UNWILLING PARTICIPANT

When a child refuses to come it is encumbent upon the parents to insist. Such insistence, in itself, has therapeutic implication. Similarly, it is encumbent upon the therapist to insist that parents succeed in this task.

For example, when the disharmony in a family is intimately linked to a child nearing emancipation who refuses to attend, the therapist can profitably call for a clarification of the child's position in the family by suggesting the following: if the child-nearing-maturity is considered a member of the family, he participates in family problem—solving activities and joins the treatment; otherwise, he leaves the home or changes his classification to that of a boarder, paying rent and being free to come and go as he wishes. Such a seemingly hard attitude can have a salutary effect on all family

23

members in the task of creating separateness with nearly adult children. Undoubtedly, this struggle would be immediately working on one part, perhaps the largest segment, of this family's presenting difficulty.

When the reluctant one is a spouse, the therapist can intervene directly by personally inviting participation for a single session, at a time convenient to the hesitant one. Then, regardless of the prevailing topics (preferably not the reluctance) the therapist tries to motivate the recalcitrant. Unwillingness to participate in family therapy is usually caused by a fear of being blamed, a sense of added personal burden, or reservations about the therapy itself. Regardless of its basis, an experience during the session of contributing something of value to the family often dissolves hesitation.

At the end of the interview, should the spouse still refuse further attendance, the therapist weighs the ultimatum against his own view of whether he can be of value to this family without the partner's presence. He can profitably explore this point with all of them and custom tailor a decision.

6. TIMING AND SCHEDULING OF INTERVIEWS

Sessions of several hours duration, appointed when specific difficulties arise, is preferable to traditional, regularly scheduled, one hour weekly interviews.

Subsequent interviews are provided for specific reasons. There are three: 1) when the session ends because of fatigue rather than problem closure; 2) to reinforce or otherwise secure the gains already achieved; or, 3) to penetrate to another level where a more stable closure can be assured.

Closure means that a family now has some problem-solving skill that can be used, at least towards resolving the concern that

24

brought them to the therapist. If the family is prepared to stop while the therapist believes that more can be accomplished to secure the family's continued successful struggling, he says so, giving particulars.

> *Therapist:* I'm glad things are going well at home with the children, but your desire to stop here worries me a bit. You don't seem to consult each other enough or trust each other sufficiently. For instance, when . . .

A thoroughgoing discussion follows which determines the fate of the therapy.

7. FAMILY THERAPY FOR THE SINGLE PERSON

Individuals living alone and without an intimate companion can beneficially be placed in a temporary family—a group. Such groups are encouraged to function as a family, meeting each other at will outside the interviews, and seriously concerning themselves with the character of their relatedness during the interviews. Reluctance to meet outside the group—much less to live together—are also pertinent topics.

When a group member gains a partner, he or she is encouraged to leave the group in favor of a free flight into the relationship. Should unrelenting difficulties arise they are advised to seek family therapy together.

2

The Interview (Procedure)

The family interview may be likened to a battlefield in which each, including the therapist, is encouraged to bring forth his most concerted effort to resolve whatever issue is at hand. However, unlike most battles, this struggle has a very special goal: the victory of each at the expense of none. The weapons are also unique: self-disclosure and the courage to be vulnerable.

The battle proper is among the family members. The issues to be settled are theirs, the struggle to be waged is among themselves. From time to time and for quite specific reasons, the therapist becomes one of the combatants, and then, the battle momentarily enlarges to include him more personally. But for the most part the struggle belongs to the family and is to be conducted within the framework of a family conversation.

The first conflict presented by the family, usually the issue that pressed them to seek therapy, is not the problem, it is a signal; a belated cry of personal anguish. For the therapist, how a family functions together is always the problem.

As a mechanic, consulted about a worrisome engine noise, revs up the engine in preference to listening to a lengthy description about its disturbing sound, the family therapist starts up a family conversation in preference to taking a history.

1. START A FAMILY CONVERSATION

A conversation among family members serves two functions. Not only does it reveal defective patterns of relating, but it also immediately puts a family into the essential vehicle for continued problem solving—the family conversation. Consequently, though initial remarks are directed to the therapist, as quickly as possible he directs their attention to one another. This is achieved by finding their differences of opinion on personal matters and urging negotiation.

> *Mother:* Our 15 year old son Jim has been making a lot of trouble for us lately.

The healthier the family, the more readily they talk to each other. For instance, should Jim respond immediately to his mother's charge with, "That's not true!", it would indicate that he has both self-confidence and the hope of being heard. Let's assume Jim doesn't leap in.

> *Therapist* (to Jim, evocatively): Do you agree that the number one problem in this family is that you are a trouble-maker?
>
> *Jim:* Not really.
>
> *Therapist:* Tell her what you think it is.
>
> *Jim:* It's no use.
>
> *Therapist* (to Mother): Do you have anything to say to his hopelessness.
>
> *Mother:* I think we've said all there is to say.

Family members are often reluctant to engage one another, particularly initially. The therapist perseveres by offering himself, if necessary.

> *Therapist* (to Jim): I'd like to know what you think is the problem, Jim.
>
> *Jim:* They're too rigid.

The battlelines often have both parents on one side. It is better when it is a free-for-all.

> *Therapist:* Both of them identical?
>
> *Jim:* Mother more than Father.
>
> *Therapist:* Then, maybe you can get some help from him.
>
> *Jim:* He's too weak. He always gives in to her.
>
> *Therapist* (to Father): Do you agree with Jim?
>
> *Father:* Of course not.
>
> *Therapist:* You didn't tell him.

The family with a persistently psychosomatic adult is one of the most difficult to start. A psychosomatic parent has the most intense personal relationship with the symptom while the rest of the family usually respects both the symptom and the relationship to it.

> *Wife:* I have these horrible headaches. I've had them ever since I can remember.
>
> *Therapist:* Who is the biggest headache in your life these days?
>
> *Wife* (smiling cooly): No one. Everything is fine at home.
>
> *Therapist:* I don't expect you to believe me, but when everything gets finer at home, your headaches will disappear. Now, tell me one thing that can be improved (usually psychosomatics will answer with something mechanical like, "Well, I could use a new dishwasher", so it is best to add) between you and your husband.
>
> *Wife:* I can't think of a thing.
>
> *Therapist:* Perhaps you can get some help from your husband.

Wife (to Husband): Can you think of anything, dear?

Husband: I think everything's fine.

Though the family clings to a united position against the therapist's perspective, there are bound to be different degrees of benefit each derive from keeping the symptom in the family. It is those differences that the therapist will tease out.

Therapist: Perfect?

Husband: Nothing's perfect.

Therapist: What's not perfect about your marriage?

Husband: Well, my wife's headaches often keep us from going places and doing things.

Therapist: And I'll bet you're a good sport about it.

Husband: She can't help it if she has headaches.

Therapist: Have you ever suspected that she uses her headaches on you?

Husband (smiling): I've thought of it.

Therapist: I'm certain of it. Take up one of those times with her right now.

"We" is an attitude—usually, without foundation—and never a fact; and is not restricted to the psychosomatic family constellation.

Wife: My mother-in-law is destroying our marriage.

Therapist (to Husband): You agree, of course.

Husband: As a matter of fact, I do. It's just that we don't know what to do about it.

Therapist: I'm sure your wife does. (Then, to the wife). Tell him.

Discord is always detectable by digging for specifics.

> *Husband:* We don't know what's wrong. We just don't have any feeling for each other any longer. We think of separating but we really don't want to.
>
> *Therapist* (to Wife): Where does your version differ?
>
> *Wife:* It doesn't.
> *Therapist* (to Husband): Tell her your fantasy of the girl who could arouse your feeling: how she would behave and what she would do that would be different from your wife's behavior.

Here is an easy one:

> *Single mother of 3 teenagers:* I can't seem to manage the children.
>
> *Therapist:* Which one first and what would you like to manage?
>
> *Mother:* Karen's smoking hash.
>
> *Therapist:* What do you want to say to her about it?
>
> *Mother:* Stop!
>
> *Therapist* (to Karen): Answer her, Karen.

Selecting a Topic

It is not necessary to begin with the topic that motivated the consultation. Any topic will do: the weather, football, politics, the difficulty of starting the interview. Family conversation is propelled on its therapeutic way by pointing towards the personal wish that invariably lives within the topic.

> *Mother:* If there were more public facilities for children, we wouldn't be here now.
>
> *Therapist* (to the rest of the family): Anyone disagree?

Should all agree or remain silent, the therapist can return to the mother for specifics.

> *Therapist* (to Mother): How would that help you solve what? And with whom?
>
> *Mother:* There is no one to stay at home with the young ones, so we fight all the time and it makes for bad feelings at home.
>
> *Therapist:* With whom do you have the most bad feeling?
>
> *Mother:* Especially with Anne, since she is the oldest.
>
> *Therapist* (to Anne): Your mother says she wants to have a better relationship with you. Any suggestions as to how she can get it?

On Taking Histories

Collecting historical facts is of doubtful value. The only possible immediate value of taking a history, if indeed it can be called that, lies in providing the therapist with a formality which frees him from his initial anxiety of meeting strangers who have expectations of him.

By allowing historical material to emerge spontaneously rather than collecting it in advance, the therapist gets to see how it is used today, thereby catapulting cold, distant and questionable data into immediate relevance.

> *She:* You never stop the children. You leave all the discipline to me and I don't like that.
>
> *He:* You know it's not easy for me. It might be different if I were their natural father and had been with them all their lives instead of just a couple of years.

The intensity of feeling about an historical fact and the readiness to explore it—both more important to the therapy than the fact itself—are more evident when permitted to emerge as part of the conversation.

31

3

He: I sometimes think I really don't love you any longer.

She: I can't stand hearing that any more. You've been telling me that ever since you had that affair last year. Why don't you just go to her and be done with it!

2. THE SEARCH FOR PERSONAL NEEDS

Longing (aliases: desire, want, need, wish, hope, etc.) is the skeleton upon which the flesh of conversation hangs. When there is no desire, conversation is hollow or absent. When the desire is not defined the conversation cannot take meaningful form. Desire, clearly expressed and movingly delivered brings change in its wake, sometimes through fulfillment, sometimes through the expression alone. Find the wants, starting with the therapist.

> What do you want and from whom?

is the therapist's everpresent question to each, including himself. It can serve as a cogent starting point for the therapy when the conversation does not flow forth spontaneously.

> I'd like to know what you would like from me today.

Or, more directly,

> What do you want from each other that you aren't getting these days?

Or, perhaps with humor (It is possible to be serious without being solemn),

> Give me one problem you all want cured today. Make it a big one as I don't like to bother with piddling ones.

32

The entire course of the therapy is characterized by a search and surface operation for the immediate desire *not yet expressed.* Desires stack like a deck of cards. The moment one is uncovered a new one lies ready to be revealed. The therapist keeps a constant vigil for the next emerging desire by modifying his original query to a watchful,

> And what do you (or to himself—I) want *now?*

When conversation becomes lost in words, the therapist can go to one member with,

> Your words blind me and I cannot see what it is you are asking for. Try to say what you want right now in one sentence—or less.

Surfacing the desires must be done in an orderly fashion. Although an experienced therapist may be able to see into the stack of back-logged desires he must guard against pulling from the bottom of the deck.

Example
A husband and wife seek help for a growing sexual incompatibility—the husband's desire continues while the wife's has essentially disappeared.

> *Therapist* (to Wife): Tell him why you no longer want to be sexual with him.

Asking why is to get quickly to specifics—the meat upon which conversation feeds—and not for the purpose of arriving at reasonable understanding.

> *Wife:* I don't know. It's just unpleasant to me now.
>
> *Therapist* (pressing): Tell him what is unpleasant about his behavior.

This opens the door for her to consider other areas of discontent (unfulfilled desires). Often the sexual arena is a minor battlefield that finally reflects a longstanding and growing incompatibility. In this instance, as will be seen, that was not the case.

> *Wife:* He seems so inconsiderate.
>
> *Therapist:* Tell him an example.
>
> *Wife* (to Husband): For instance, you often hurt me when we are sexual.
>
> *Husband* (innocently): Really? I never knew that. Why didn't you ever tell me?
>
> *Wife:* I have tried but you just tell me I'm too inhibited or overly sensitive.
>
> *Husband* (chuckling): Reminds me of the joke where the guy says to the girl while they're doing it, "Did I hurt you?" and she says, "No. Why do you ask?" and he says, "Because you moved." (He laughs.)
>
> *She:* I'd like you to take me seriously.
>
> *He:* I do. But I think you're just too sexually inhibited.

She brings him a serious desire—not to be abused sexually—which he merely deflects by changing the subject from pain to prudishness. At the top of the husband's deck of desires the therapist sees a desire to hide his next underlying desire: a wish to be sexually cruel. And beneath that one, the therapist may visualize a desire to express the frustration of earlier sexual disappointments (not necessarily with her). And below that he may envision an original longing for loving intimacy. The therapist must not pull from the bottom of the deck by saying sympathetically to the husband, for instance,

> I can see from your cavalier attitude that you must have had great longings for sex and affection that were frustrated. Perhaps you can tell your wife about them, now.

34

The husband, not yet at that deeper level, is likely to leap at the chance to escape the necessary and painful step by step unravelling of backlogged desires (pain roughly equivalent to the unexpressed pain originally bypassed), and answer with affectless understanding,

> Well, yes, I've had my share of frustration like anyone else, I suppose. Are you saying that has something to do with my present attitude?

The best that can come from such premature surfacing is some understanding—and a continued desire to be sexually cruel.

Preferably, the therapist works from the top of the stack, focusing on the immediate and he disregards his farsighted and profound interpretations. With this husband, for instance, the therapist could simply call attention to his lighthearted attitude, or his diversionary tactic of changing the subject. Or, if the therapist believes the husband is almost ready to acknowledge the apparent immediate desires, he can suggest,

> *Therapist:* Sometimes a man enjoys hurting a woman sexually but is ashamed to admit it. Does that fit at all for you?
>
> *Husband:* I've never thought about it. Well, in a way I have. I've had fantasies (then, hastily to his wife) but I don't want to hurt you.

Cure lies in self-disclosure. It is the revelation of distorted desire that releases.

> *Therapist:* Tell her some of your cruel fantasies (Your desire to hurt.)

The therapist can expect objections. The husband might say that he dare not or the wife may say that she does not want to know them.

Suppose, as the husband begins to unveil his punishing pictures, his wife comes with a counter desire:

> *Wife:* Please! Don't tell me. I don't want to hear them. Just the idea that you have such thoughts frightens me.

The therapist's task remains the same: to surface and confront emerging desires.

> *Therapist* (to silent Husband): What do you want to say now?
>
> *Husband:* I don't know. I begin to see your point. But I don't want to hurt her, either.
>
> *Therapist:* Tell her
>
> *Husband:* I really don't want to hurt you, hon, but I feel like it might do me some good to get this stuff out in the open. I've been joking about it long enough.
>
> *Wife:* But I'm frightened.

Whether or not the fantasies are revealed is unimportant. They are now only a topic. The search for ways to reconcile emerging and often conflicting personal desires is the task.

When The Therapist Doesn't Want To Know
Sometimes, more often than is readily admitted, the therapist is preoccupied and would not like to know immediately what a family wants. To wend his way to the starting line, he declares where he is.

> I like your coat. Where did you get it? Was it expensive?

If such thoughts are embarrassing, the therapist can preamble with,

> I know you came here for more important matters, but before we begin, I'd like to ask about that coat you are wearing. I like it and wondered

The therapist's attention may be elsewhere. Sometimes, saying something about it is sufficient to dispel a minor distraction.

> I'm getting hungry. (Looking at his watch.) I hope I can make it until lunchtime. (He listens seriously for a moment for the impact of his words on himself.) Yes, I think I can make it.

Sometimes, saying it isn't enough. Then, more deliberate action may be necessary. He may reach into a drawer and pull out a box of crackers, taking one while offering some to his guests. He may ask if anyone else would like a cup and then phone out for coffee before starting the session.

His distraction may be more difficult to dispel. Then, depending upon his own comfort and capability, he may talk with the family awhile about his preoccupation.

> I am still thinking about my last interview. It was quite moving and in a way I'm still there with them. I enjoy my work but it is not always easy for me to jump in and out of families according to the clock. I don't have anything else I needed to tell them. It was just a nice feeling we had together and if I could have chosen, I would have just sat with them a bit longer. (Slowly, his attention may arrive.) I suppose it's a long way from the way you feel with each other just now. (Or, perhaps) Does it bother you to hear me babble this way?

When the therapist becomes distracted or disinterested after the interview has begun, he explores his immediate experience with this family for what it is that he wants and isn't getting. His specific desire—or distress, if negatively perceived—is taken promptly to the family member who arouses it. The therapist's desires—or lack of them—exert a crucial influence. They are best kept in the open.

3. REFINING THE MESSAGE

Where the issue of desire concerns itself largely with immediacy (*Now* what do you want?), refining the message concerns itself largely with specificity (Now what do you *precisely* want and from whom?). Change the vague to the definite, the abstract to the concrete, the general to the specific, the negative to the positive, the outdated to the immediate. And most important, change we to I.

> *Mother:* We need to communicate better.
> *Therapist:* Who won't do as you say?
>
> *Father:* I think we should be kinder to each other.
> *Therapist:* Who isn't kind to you, for instance?
>
> *Father* (to his family): I just want a little more peace at home.
> *Therapist:* Tell them your terms.

Specificity can be sought from the sender or the receiver.

> *Wife:* I wish you would show some interest towards me once in awhile.
>
> *Husband:* I do.
>
> *Wife:* I don't feel it.
>
> *Husband:* Maybe *that's* the problem.
>
> *Wife:* Maybe it is, but I still don't feel it.
>
> *Husband:* Well, that's not my problem.
>
> *Therapist* (to Husband): I'm wondering if you know exactly what she is asking for.
>
> *Husband:* Not exactly.
>
> *Therapist:* You could ask her.

Messages delivered with discordant nonverbal behavior are to be refined.

> *Husband* (Looking and sounding rather resigned): I don't see what's wrong with things as they are. Nothing can be perfect.

Therapist: You don't sound satisfied with them yourself.

Husband: I'm not.

Therapist: You left that part out.

Husband: I don't think that's important.

Therapist: Your dissatisfactions are more important than your philosophy.

As with discordant nonverbal behavior, when attitudes contradict the expressed desire, they are confronted.

Husband (to wife): You are always so dependent on me, I don't like it. You live in my shadow. You don't think for yourself. I wish you were more independent.

Wife: I think a more serious problem for me which I'd like to discuss is our sex life.

Husband: That's not the problem. That's only a symptom of it. The problem is your dependency.

Wife: Maybe. But sex is still a problem for me that I'd like to discuss with you.

Husband: Discussing that would be a waste of time.

Process confrontations are generally preferable to content comments. Here, although the therapist may agree with the husband's viewpoint, his attitude is discordant with his expressed desire and is to be challenged.

Therapist (to husband): You ask for your wife's independent thought, yet when she offers it you summarily dismiss it.

The therapist must persevere.

14 year old to parents: You all don't understand anything.

Father: That's what you tell us whenever we object to anything you do.

39

14 year old: Not true.

Therapist (to 14 year old): Specifics please.

14 year old: You all don't understand my friends.

Father: You mean we don't like some of them. That's true.

Therapist (again to 14 year old): Tell him what he doesn't understand about your friends.

14 year old: That they have different values.

Therapist: For instance.

14 year old: They think it's o.k. to smoke hash.

Therapist: And you?

14 year old: I think it's o.k., too.

Therapist: For you or them?

14 year old: Both.

The 14 year old is approaching specificity. He wants his parents approval for his hash smoking. Now the parents objecting message similarly requires definition before their conversation can proceed.

Therapist (to Father): Your position?

Father: I said it. I object.

Therapist: Specifics, please.

Father need not give reasons. He could simply refuse. This refusal then becomes the specific position to which the boy, the therapist, and the mother can respond.

Wants must be forthright, specific, personal—and preferably, petty and practical. (See Chapter 4, Sections 3 and 5.)

I want you to make your bed daily.

and not imploringly,

Why can't you be more responsible?

> I refuse (don't want) to call your mother every week and feign interest.

and not self-effacingly,

> It would be nice if I weren't the one who had to call your mother all the time.

> I need more household money.

and not pitifully,

> It's so hard to make ends meet. It seems there is never quite enough to cover. Prices are . . .

> I don't like criticism, your's or anyone's, now or ever. Say what you want but don't pick, pick, pick!

and not vaguely,

> It seems like you are never satisfied with me.

> I won't stop talking just because you tell me to shut up.

and not deceptively,

> When you talk to me that way I don't know what to say to you.

The deepest personal desires (e.g., the desire to be loved) cannot, of course, be commanded or specifically negotiated. However, through the expression and negotiation of the petty, the practical, the ordinary desires of daily living one discovers what is possible and also improves chances for deeper satisfactions.

4. THE PROMPT, POIGNANT DELIVERY

Direct all ready remarks to their proper target, the person they concern. All remarks about one person spoken to a third party are considered gossip and undesirable. (See Chapter 4, section 2.)

"Tell 'em," is the password.

Wife (to therapist about Husband): I don't know how to convince him that we really need him.

Therapist: Tell him *that.*

Often the steps mingle.

Wife: I've tried. He doesn't understand.

Therapist: Be specific. Tell him what you need him for.

Again, persistence is usually required.

Wife: I've tried, but it's so difficult to be specific about such things. It's more than things like support and help around the house.

Therapist: Tell him *that.*

While the message slowly changes (deepens), the therapist persists.

Wife: I've tried but I feel hopeless.

Therapist: Tell him.

Should the wife look at her husband and begin to cry, for instance, her message of desire for him is completed and his response, if not spontaneously forthcoming, is invited.

Therapist (to Husband): She is talking to you and you do not answer.

Remarks rerouted to their proper destination are often watered down to questions or talking about (making a topic of the message instead of delivering it).

Husband (to therapist): I hate it when my wife tells me to help discipline the children and then complains that I do it too harshly.

Therapist: Tell her.

Husband (to Wife): Why do you do it?

Therapist: That's not what you were saying to me. You told me you hated it. You weren't wondering why she did it.

Husband (to Wife): I do hate it. You know I do. (Gathering momentum) Dammit! I want you to butt out when I discipline the kids.

The husband has delivered his message clearly, poignantly. It is a good beginning or conclusion. The choice is his wife's.

Should a family member be unable to deliver a message which the therapist considers worthwhile, the therapist can play Mercury and bridge the gap.

16 year old: They just think I'm stupid.

Therapist: Doesn't that hurt?

16 year old (shrugs): Sometimes.

Therapist: Tell them.

16 year old: They aren't interested.

Therapist: Sometimes parents need to be reminded that their kids need their interest and appreciation. That's your job. Tell them.

16 year old: It's useless.

Therapist: I think it's difficult, but not useless. (Turning to parents:) Assume he said all this to you and answer him.

Sometimes, a response is diverted to the therapist. For instance, a wife's serious and challenging confrontations are evaded by her husband.

Therapist: You haven't answered your wife, again.

Husband: Damn! You never give up, do you?

Therapist: You still haven't answered her.

43

Frustration towards the therapist for his perseverance (and other things) is appropriate and welcome. However, the therapist must continue to guard against evasion.

This husband now speaks directly to his wife, but uses the intervention as a conversation piece. Interventions are to be applied or refuted, never discussed.

> *Husband* (to Wife): Doc's right, honey. Often, I don't answer you.

> *Therapist* (to Husband): You still haven't answered her.

A message properly delivered includes the associated affect (See Chapter 3, section 4). The meaninglessness of "I love you" delivered dispassionately is obvious to all. When the message is a negative one, however, there is a tendency to encourage dissociation.

I hate you!	Must you say that with such venom!?
I can't bear the way we are living together.	Can't you stop crying so that we can talk about it reasonably?

Generally, the words are information for the listener while the affect (the music) is needed relief for the sender. Both words and music are essential for the optimal delivery. (See Chapter 3, section 6.)

When The Target Is Not A Family Member
Sometimes, during an exchange between family members, a clear message is uncovered that belongs to someone else. When that person is living and reachable, such as a neighbor, co-worker, friend, or relative, personal delivery becomes part of homework and is not to be gossiped away in the therapy.

The therapist is ever alert for remarks that are for him.

> *Husband* (to Wife): We don't seem to be making much progress, lately.

44

Wife: That's true.

Therapist: Whom do you think we should hold responsible for that? You, your wife, or me?

Husband: Oh, we all are, of course.

Therapist: Tell each of us, starting with me, how you think we might do better.

Here, since the therapist is a direct target, in addition to his guidance he will respond personally. (See chapter 5 part 2.)

When the recipient for a message is a deceased relative, a dialogue can be arranged by using one of the Gestalt 'there and now' techniques, beginning, for instance, with

> Go to your father now. Be with him. Talk to him.

Or,

> Close your eyes and see if you can be with him, now. Speak with him, aloud.

Sometimes, the message is for oneself. Then, a self-confronting dialogue is structured with the individual speaking both parts, alternately, until, as with any other encounter, the conflict is resolved (See Chapter 5 for elaboration of incountering).

5. A TIME FOR RESPONSE

At home, reactions may be necessarily delayed. Practical details may intervene, such as the need for a child to get to school on time, or by the arrival of unexpected guests; or, one may simply refuse to continue a discussion at that moment with no reason beyond a personal desire to detach for awhile. Postponements at home can be advantageous. They often provide valuable cooling off periods during a difficult and protracted controversy. However, during the therapeutic interview, a delayed response is generally considered an absent response—a tactic of tarrying—and is to be challenged immediately. During therapy distractions are purposely minimized and the heat of frustration is to be used for the fire needed to forge new relatedness.

Responses are to meet all the requirements prescribed above for sponses. In addition, they are to be, with rare exception, prompt, timely, to the point and full blown.

Premature responses—interruptions—are generally disruptive and are to be discouraged. When it is rare and in the heat of battle, a simple, "Wait a minute. Let her finish." is sufficient. When interruptions are a common event they require more deliberate attention. Then, both parties are asked to monitor their own side. To the interruptor,

> You did it again.

To the interrupted,

> And you allow it.

Vigor may be necessary in a talkative family in which interrupting has been a long-standing style.

> Shut up all of you and listen to me. This constant interrupting must go. I won't stand for it. I expect each of you to become your own mouth monitor immediately. Talk one at a time and let each finish.

Monitoring their monitoring may be the therapist's appropriate preoccupation for awhile.

Interrupting long-winded and seemingly pointless monologues are, of course, appropriate. An invitation for a brief summary simultaneously offers guidance.

Stop talking a minute. I'm lost. What's your point? In one brief sentence.

It is also appropriate to interrupt to inform a person of disinterest.

> *Therapist* (interrupts daughter and speaks to Mother): You don't seem interested in what your daughter is saying.
>
> *Mother:* I'm not.
>
> *Therapist:* Then have the courtesy to tell her. (And to the daughter:) Either insist on her attention or don't talk, but don't waste your breath.

Response must be to the point.

> *Wife:* You seem so irritable all the time.
>
> *Husband:* You're no box of cheer, yourself.
>
> *Therapist* (to Husband): You can take that up with her next. The current topic is *your* irritability, not hers.

Although to the point, response must not mask the personal message.

> *Same husband as above* (to wife): You're right. I am irritable much of the time.
>
> *Therapist:* Now your voice has become flat. All the life has gone out of it.
>
> *Husband:* Well, naturally, I don't like what she's saying, even though it's true.
>
> *Therapist:* You didn't tell her that part.
>
> *Husband* (to wife): Well, I don't.
>
> *Therapist:* Your voice is still dead.
>
> *Husband* (becoming obviously distressed): But, if I show her

47

how annoyed I feel, she'll accuse me of being irritable, again. I don't know what to do.

Therapist: You could tell her that.

When response is not spontaneously forthcoming, it is invited.

Could you respond?

What's going on inside of you right now?

I noticed you shrugged. What are you saying with it?

If all fails, the sender may be invited to react to the silent response or other members of the family may be invited to contribute.

Commonly, responses are forthcoming but are vague and circumstantial, requiring the same corrective attention as described earlier. When the listener is obviously evasive the evasiveness is confronted.

Wife: We must do something about Marcia's fear of you. Perhaps if you stopped screaming at her all the time, it would help.

Husband: It might.

If the spouse doesn't pick up on the evasion the therapist points it out to one or both of them. To the husband, for example, he might say, evocatively,

That's no answer. Tell her what you think of her accusation.

Or, to the wife,

Are you satisfied with his answer?

Wife: Of course not!

Therapist: How should he know? You didn't tell him.

Another example:

> *Wife:* I wish you'd stay home more.
>
> *Husband:* You know how busy I am at the office, especially now. This is our season.

In this instance, she is vague, he is evasive. Either or both can be confronted to intensify the work.

Suppose all attempts to elicit a verbal response fail. The therapist can then go to the topic and participate more personally in the needed discussion.

Example

Mother has expressed concern about Barbara's (age 16) new boyfriend who has a police record for selling hash. Barbara has protested, swearing that he is not a big time dope peddler but only a good guy caught in the hysteria of the times. Mother has turned to Father, who is characteristically unresponsive, and expressed her wish that he would say something. He looks thoughtful, shrugs his shoulders almost imperceptibly, and says nothing.

> *Therapist:* What are you thinking?
>
> *Father:* Nothing.
>
> *Therapist:* You shrugged. It means something.

Silence.

> *Therapist:* Does it?
>
> *Father:* I didn't notice that I shrugged.
>
> *Therapist:* O.k. But I'm sure you have an opinion about the boyfriend issue even if it's that you think the issue isn't worth bothering with. I'd like to hear your opinion.
>
> *Father:* I don't know the boy.

Therapist: Are you saying you'd like to meet him?

Father: I don't know if that would help.

Therapist: Would you rather your wife and Barbara settle this matter without bothering you with it?

Father: They aren't bothering me. I just don't have any suggestions.

The therapist believes the father and concludes that Father's inability to have personal opinions is deeply rooted and that the current issue cannot wait for Father's personality reorganization.

Therapist (to Mother): I believe your husband has given you all he can for now. I'd suggest that you invite the boy over some evening and get acquainted with him. (To Father:) It will give you a chance to find out if meeting him would help you to form an opinion which your wife would welcome. (And then to Mother:) Then you can talk with the boy about your concerns about his police record. It would be better if your position were based on your personal opinion of the boy rather than on information about the boy. (And then to Barbara:) What do you think of my suggestion?

When the immediate issue is dispatched, the therapist might well return to the parents (with his desire) to discuss the heavier issue of the great distance between what Mother desires in the way of participation from Father and what Father can actually provide. The issue is not simply Father's retiring personality but the distance between Mother and Father. It is for the struggle about that distance to decide what elements are to be reckoned with. His immediate behavior as well as her's and the therapist's will shape the course of the battle and determine its outcome.

When Response Is Unnecessary
In the wake of expressed desire there sometimes comes a new realization—perhaps recognition that the desire could never be

fulfilled with this particular person. Then, one's own crying completes the message.

Sometimes the personal message needs only to be delivered. The expression itself is complete and response is welcome but optional. (See Chapter 4, section 7.) The Bible provides a ready example:

> Then Joseph could not refrain himself . . . . (and) made himself known unto his brethren . . . And he wept aloud . . . . And Joseph said unto his brethren, I am Joseph . . . . And he fell upon his brother Benjamin's neck, and wept: and Benjamin wept . . . .
>
> Genesis 45:1, 3, 14

6. MONITORING THE FAMILY CONVERSATION

The sequential steps that form the subheadings of this chapter are like the notes of a musical scale. One must first see their harmonic relatedness; then, as with the learned scale they are lost from consciousness to form the invisible scaffolding for improvised interviewing that begins and ends wherever it sounds best.

Pursuing the ongoing conversation requires skill in focusing on the immediate, which can be learned without too much difficulty; and, a perspective that discerns what in that immediate is the most penetrating issue to focus upon; a capability which depends on the therapist's own personal development and comes largely from his own experiences.

Focusing On The Immediate
The therapist does not live in the here and now, as is often touted, but rather uses the immediate as a window through which he peers in search of his next move.

Once an interaction has begun, the task of pursuing it is achieved by seeing that the combatants stand toe to toe (mouth to ear and ear to mouth) in mutual self-disclosure until immediate desires are met or supplanted. An initial interview illustrates.

Thirteen year old Carol forcibly signals her family that all is not well at home by overdecorating. Her bright lipstick smeared with careful exaggeration onto a silly smile and her eye shadow which overshadows her whole countenance compete for visibility through a veil of well-combed hair. Her clothes suggest more the harlequin than the vampire. Father with an equally absurd smile greets the therapist with, "As you can see, we're having quite a problem with Carol."

Combatants are invited front and center.

> *Therapist* (to Carol): I'm sure you don't agree with the way he puts it, do you?
>
> *Carol shakes her giggly head and says nothing. I think she is crazy.*
>
> *Therapist* (again to Carol): I'd be more interested in your problems with them.
>
> *Carol says nothing but her giggling slows to a thoughtful smile. I register her response and elect not to press her further at this time.*

Speak to each rather than to several at once.

> *Therapist* (to Father): I suppose you believe you've tried everything.
>
> *Father* (still smiling): Yes, we have.
>
> *Therapist* (to Mother): Everything?
>
> *Mother:* I don't know what else we could do.

Anchor in practical reality rather than ideas.

> *Therapist:* You could take the lipstick and eye makeup off her.
>
> *I notice Carol's sober interest.*

Mother: We've tried but she objects.

Therapist: Did you expect her to cooperate?

Mother: But she gets so violent.

Therapist: Get help from your husband.

Father (to Therapist, still smiling): When I start to use force she (the mother) stops me.

Mother (weakly): I can't stand aggression.

Before Carol can be faced by her parents, they must face each other. The therapist sees more readiness to engage in the father's posture, facial expression and spontaneous disclosures. Be lazy. Always move the easiest one first.

Therapist (to Father): Sounds like you know best what to do. I suggest you quit smiling and insist on your way.

Engagement is being recommended, not violence. Sometimes violence is part of needed engagement for a while. It is better to meet it than to abandon the child.

Father (to Therapist): When my wife would complain that she couldn't get Carol out of bed in the morning, I'd go up, take the covers off and pull her out of bed. She'd struggle and my wife would stop me.

All remarks are present tense. His reversion to a story from the past is saying somthing like, "I don't dare tackle my wife *now.*"

Prefer action to analysis.

Therapist: I still think you know best and should insist.

Father (looking seriously at his wife): What do you think?

Mother: I'm afraid of what will happen. She gets so destructive.

Father falls silent. He appears to be a man who can smile sub-missively or get violent, but who knows little about the enorm-ous world of negotiating that lies between those extremes. I choose to prop him up for further negotiation by talking to the wife and setting an example rather than cajoling the father to carry on when he seems so inexperienced.

Therapist (to Mother): You talk as though she is not being destructive at this moment. Carol is at war with you. Her war paint should tell you that. That she gets self-destructive instead of telling you how much she hates you and needs you shouldn't fool you.

Father (encouraged, carries on): I've never thought of it that way but I think he's right.

Mother: It sounds right.

Do not allow interventions to become conversation pieces.

Since the conversation between the parents is degenerating any-way, I decide to invite Carol's active verbal participation again, both to let her know she is always welcome and also to sound her out.

Therapist: Do you think I'm crazy, Carol?

Carol gives me an angry flash, nods and then retreats to giggling again.

Therapist: And I think you're a bit crazy, too, when you giggle and make yourself ugly instead of telling what you don't like.

Carol stares at me and then looks away without giggling. She has heard and I know she is ready to meet her parents.

Therapist (this time to Father instead of Mother): Now what?

Father (anger rising): I'm thinking of all the times she has stopped me.

54

Don't stand in the way of the intervention by saying, for instance, "I see that your anger is rising. You are angry with her now. Tell her all the things you are angry about." Such remarks invite self-consciousness and reduce the participant to a puppet. Guidance is best when it points but does not precisely prescribe.

> *Therapist:* Talk to her.
>
> *Father* (to Mother): I've saved up so damn much anger. Not just about Carol. You stop *me,* too. All of us. We never fight. We never shout. We never solve anything. Damn!
>
> *Mother cowers in silence.*

The therapist must bring her up to the battle line. He does it kindly or challengingly varying with what he believes will serve best with the least effort. Again, laziness is his guide.

> *Therapist* (encouraging Mother): Answer him.
>
> *Mother:* I'm afraid for what will happen.
>
> *Father:* You're always afraid for what will happen. We've got to risk it. We can't let her go on like this.
>
> *Mother:* But what if she breaks things as she's done before?
>
> *Father:* We must stop her.
>
> *Mother:* I don't know if I can bear it.
>
> *Therapist* (believing Mother can): You have no choice. (And then to Father:) Do you think you can fight both of them simultaneously?
>
> *Father* (with conviction): I think so.
>
> *Throughout this conversation I have watched Carol. Her initial restlessness is gone. Her giggling is replaced by sobriety. I conclude that Carol's non-verbal behavior is a sign of recognition and deep appreciation for what is happening.*

Once the direction is indicated and there is evidence of serious intention, action is preferred to further discussion. The therapist can suggest the arena: either, the parents can be challenged to see that Carol's war paint is removed before the interview is completed or it can be stated as a condition for the next visit, providing them with a little more time to negotiate with Carol.

> *Therapist:* I suggest we stop here. You know what must be done. (To Carol:) Do you have anything to say to me or to your parents, Carol?

> *As expected, Carol does not answer.*

> *Therapist* (to Carol): I think you have done the right thing, Carol, by calling attention to the difficulties in your family. It's unfortunate that you have had to do it in such a self-destructive way, but it's impossible for kids to do it any other way when parents don't teach them how. (Carol's full comprehension of the message is not essential.)

Should the therapist have any residuals, he reveals them.

> *Therapist* (to Father): I believe you can do it. I do not share your wife's concern about you. I think you can be firm without being unduly severe or punishing. (To Mother) I see your fear more a consequence of inexperience than because you are weak or truly fearful. Some struggle in this family will be refreshing (Then to both) Remember, this is only step one. It is not enough to force and fight Carol. She also must be heard. You have yet to discover what she hates about living in this family. We only know one thing so far that she must hate: having to be self-destructive instead of being able to tell you her anger and disagreements. Opposing her self-destructiveness with vigor is the starting point. This is not a matter for discussion. Next comes listening to her and talking over other matters. (This map of things to come is the therapist's expressed wish. Response is invited.) Any questions or disagreement?

Whether the therapist comes on as a tour de force (as above) or almost imperceptibly like a gentle summer breeze depends on what, as he sees it, is called for. His job is to be effective and the full range of his personality is his equipment.

The Therapist's Perspective

Acumen comes largely from experience, particularly that which is to become part of spontaneous behavior. The questions that follow and the ensuing example are offered more to arouse the therapist's perspective than to teach it.

Along the entire path of engaging clear desire and personal response, the therapist remains ever alert for the issue that may take precedence. Does expressing the desire extinguish the desire thus making response superfluous? Does the expression of it intensify it? Does it lead to the awareness of a deeper wish? Does the response finish the subject? Or, is it the starting point for negotiations?

Is the heated discussion necessary to unload backlogged frustration in preparation for serious negotiation, or is the argument merely useless bickering that increases frustration? When the frustration from earlier suppression is relieved by venting spleen, such as a child vehemently saying, "I hate that everything has to be done *your* way and when *you* want it done" (though it be grossly exaggerated), does the issue dissolve or does it need further discussion?

Are both satisfied with the conclusions reached? Is mutual satisfaction necessary? A child may agree to accept a chore or house rule but need not like it. Between adults the opposite prevails. During a dialogue, does a third member become restless? Is the ongoing too sensitive and too personal to recognize a third member at that moment? Does closure between two disturb a third? Is lack of closure a good thing here? Who does that disturb? Shall something be done about that or is it best to let it stand so that each can get accustomed to valuable separateness?

When a third enters a fray, is the support needed? Does it deprive someone of the chance to struggle for himself? Is the loyalty to be decried? Admired? Admired, yet stopped? Does the participation of the third party change the issue significantly? Is it an interrupting distraction or does it deepen the ongoing? Does it give the third a needed feeling of participation that makes what they say of lesser concern?

Example

Mother and father are in agreement. Father has delivered their desires loud and clear to their 14 year old daughter, Sandy, who in turn has bargained effectively for the limits she wants. The final verdict: Sandy makes up her bed before leaving for school each morning; she does the dishes three days each week (and not every night); she is to be in bed by 10 pm on school nights (and not 9 pm as her parents originally suggested); and her allowance is increased to meet her growing personal needs. Sandy has grumbled gloriously and accepted the terms in proper reluctant fashion, appropriate for her 14 years. It is clear to all that her reluctance masks a secret satisfaction that is best left unspoken.

The immediate is always abundantly filled with ongoing phenomena, with what is and is not happening. The therapist waits searchingly. His awareness samples the atmosphere of the immediate. He notices a furrow on mother's brow as he simultaneously recalls her relative passivity (previously considered insignificant) during the negotiations with Sandy. He invites the furrow's message.

> *Therapist:* You seem less than contented, Mother. What are you thinking?
>
> *Mother:* It's the way he talks to Sandy.
>
> *Therapist:* Please talk to him about it.
>
> *Mother* (to her husband): I appreciate your firmness with Sandy. I could never argue with her the way you do. And I know what you tell her is right. But there's something

about the way you say it that troubles me. Sometimes it sounds like you really hate her. I know you don't. I don't know what else to say about it.

The therapist again meanders through the immediate. Does Sandy get sad, indicating that mother has spoken for her, also? Does father respond with sadness or denial, indicating that he has been touched by mother's words? Does mother's expression relieve her? or, does it intensify something within her that needs further elaboration? Does a son, silent and on the sidelines until now, wince at mother's words?

Suppose, as he looks about, the therapist sees a reaction in everyone that deserves his attention. From the many possibilities he selects one. The one he chooses will depend on the shape of his own world at that moment. Which one is he? The mother? The father? The daughter? The son? Wherever his own deepest sympathies lie, there will he go and that will be the right place for him.

3

Theory

1. THE PROCESS: TWO POINTS AND A HAPPENING

Isaac Newton started with two points in space, happened an apple between them and formulated the law of gravity. Someone else began with the moon and the earth, observed the happenings of the ocean's edge in relation to them, and explained tides. Aristotle took opposing views as his two points and, with argument as the happening, postulated the law of dialectics. These men knew what they were doing. Yet, in another sense, they didn't. They were processing.

Until quite recently, the term process was applied rather loosely, referring to anything undergoing change. Now we know that nothing is static, that all is in motion, and the term is defined more precisely. A process, composed of 2 points and something happening between them, is a dynamic yardstick; a special method for observing, describing and labelling bits and pieces of a universe in ferment—a way of bringing the world about us into comprehensible range. A process does more than measure the distance between here and there; it tells us what here and there are doing with each other.

Hegel refined Aristotle's work, saying that any thought (thesis) implied its own equal and opposite thought (antithesis), and when these two specific points were confronted, they united (synthesis) to become a single point (thesis) in a new spiral of thesis-antithesis-synthesis. This endless happening, he postulated, was the fundamental process of reality.

Now, we know that Hegel's actual discovery, regardless of any other implications it may have, was none other than the fundamental process of the mind itself, the process by which the mind orders the universe and, by so doing, brings it into comprehensible range. Hegel was looking at himself in a mirror that he called reality. He didn't know that he had glimpsed the process of processes: awareness.

2. AWARENESS: THE PROCESS OF PROCESSES

The art of processing, then, is not some clever invention of men's minds, but rather a *re-minding*, a realization, a bringing into consciousness of the mind's own inherent mechanism for orienting Man in his earthbound existence. The implication is enormous. By studying the process of awareness, laws governing all processes are discovered.

Gestalt Psychology, recognizing the process of awareness as this remarkable telescopic window between man and his universe, reversed the operation—instead of looking out through the window, it looked in. By turning awareness on itself, camp was readied for the long trek of discovering man's influence on his own happenings.

Much has been learned since Hegel's day. For instance, all objects have a gravitational or magnetic pull (called love or desire when in reference to people), and it is this inherent power of attraction that largely influences the happening and ultimate fate of processes. Also known, is that synthesis, or union, is not the only possible consequence. Escape from orbit and movement into constellation with a third point is also a possible sequence. Additionally, there are moments when the desire for cohesion is greater than the forces for adhesion, as when a drop of water lands on an oiled surface, and then there is separateness, not synthesis.

Significant among the many important discoveries about awareness, and of particular importance to the Gestalt family therapist, is the influence of the very process of becoming aware. In its memorable portrayal of the dawn of awareness—the now famous apple incident of Adam and Eve—the Bible decisively reveals that awareness itself has serious and far reaching consequences. The awareness of themselves (". . . and they knew they were naked." Genesis 3:7) immediately inspired the act of covering and also brought in its wake a host of other consequences: consequences which were attributed to God (they hadn't learned yet about processes) and from which some sources claim we are still suffering. In more immediate terms, when all know the hand is in the cookie jar—even if approved—the theft loses its zest. Awareness itself is influential.

Since knowledge of other processes can be learned by studying the process of awareness, and since the family therapist is largely concerned with the processes of growth and repair (re-growth), a look at how awareness grows can be profitable. Awareness does not grow by collecting large quantities of data and rapidly sorting them (like computers—which do not grow). Nor does awareness grow by reason. Awareness grows leisurely and thoughtlessly by processing items two by two; by dancing to and fro between two points until satisfied; and in familiar psychological jargon, by experiencing.

For example, an infant's awareness, motivated by a nascent desire to grow, sees a small stone. With the stone as one point and the fingers as the other, awareness plays with it, feels it. Then, the stone and the mouth become the points and tasting is the happening. Next the stone, the arm and throwing. Awareness plays until satisfied and then moves on. Awareness has learned from experience; awareness has grown.

Experience is the key to growth and re-growth and to the therapeutic process. Not familiar or repetitious experience. Not impersonal or educational experiences. But intimate experiences which bring in their wake new awareness. If thought is father to the deed, then awareness is its mother and experience its ultimate source of wisdom.

Gestalt therapy directs its attention to experiences that stimulate awareness—to new experiences that remind.

3. THE POINTS: YOU AND I

With himself as one point, Man's earliest thoughts about his own existence, placed the other point outside of his collective self, either in an invisible God or Spirit, or in a visible force, such as the Sun. The influence was unilateral and the other point had it. God influenced Man: Man did not influence God. Man tried. Animals were frequently sacrificed. The Aztecs profferred selected hearts of their own young. Swedish farmers sprinkled coins on the fields and Vikings offered sailors to the sea. Sometimes sacrifice worked, sometimes not. But the aspect of interest here was not the success or failure of the activity but rather the fact that the activity was primarily one of appeasement and not reciprocity. Man did not consider himself important to God and acted more out of fear than loving dedication. Man saw himself as a hopeless victim, an obsequious beggar hoping for a charitable handout.

Gradually, Man begins to appreciate his own potential and currently he often wages hot debate over where, in fact, the power lies. At one extreme remain those who feel victimized and helpless against life, while at the other pole are the metaphysicists who proclaim that each man is God and therefore is, indeed, the all powerful influence in his own happening.

Emerging from this wide range of concepts is the Humanistic movement with its suspicion that, in some remarkable way, and regardless of the conceptual power struggle in the cosmos, the two crucial points in the happening of Man are both human.

In the infancy of psychology, when this suspicion first arose, attention went, understandably, to the mother and her infant.

63

Knowledge of processes was still primitive and influence was still seen as unilateral. The mother, like God or the Sun, influenced the helpless infant. Reciprocity, the undulating to and fro feedback mechanism inherent in all processes, was largely overlooked. The baby's influence on the mother was all but ignored, and her behavior, if she was lucky enough to have it considered at all, was attributed to influences from her own childhood.

Psychology has moved along, perhaps into its own adolescence, and now considers the reciprocity between mother and child. More than that, it now strongly suspects that reciprocity in relatedness, more than such things as kindness, caring and generosity, carries the greatest influence on human behavior. A child who experiences his reciprocal importance to the family grows mighty while other children are gifted into insignificance or carefully cared for into a sense of worthlessness.

The demands of young children are simple and to the point. They ask to be seen and to be needed. "Watch me!" and "Let me do it!" are their bywords. Though one may argue that the potential for influencing the happenings in one's own life is held within each individual, at least one other person is required for it's release (realization, reminding). That fact is dictated by the process of awareness. When richly filled with the treasures of relatedness, it is increasingly possible to become both points in one's own happening. However, when attempted or forced prematurely, the result is idle, fragmented reverie, and insatiable contact hunger. There is no substitute for the personal needed other.

4. OUR HAPPENING: SEPARATING AND UNIFYING

Relatedness is often considered optional. It isn't. We are related. The question is not if, but how. The extremes of relatedness are separateness and unity. Separateness is a dimension of relatedness, not a disruption of it.

The endless search for our optimal relatedness may manifest as a struggle between a mother and daughter about a proper bedtime, siblings debating who will put the milk away, a husband and wife discussing extramarital sex, lovers ecstatically embracing, a wife crying the death of her husband. Nor is the activity limited to family. From the neighborhood squabbles of children to the challenging task of diplomats at the United Nations, all endeavor is characterized by the endlessly undulating desire for separateness and unity.

From conception, differentiation and separation appear to characterize the main thrust of human development: cells differentiate and separate, newborns differentiate and break their umbilical ties, children mature and leave the home of their parents. Yet in each instance the result leads not to a durable separateness, but to a higher order of union. Cells differentiate and separate only to cling to other cells, creating organs which, in turn, unify to establish the total organism; the newborn infant immediately rejoins its mother in a renewed union, albeit qualitatively different; and the matured child leaves his parent family to form another, more lasting unity—his own family.

Similarly, union leads to differentiation and separateness. A union between a man and a woman can create the most remarkable differentiated separateness—a child. The newborn, reunited in suckling, separates from the nipple when satisfied. A child given the proper union with its mother is eager to run out and play, to separate. A couple, successfully united, provide each other the needed ingredients for further growth and personal development (differentiated separateness). When the happening is successful separation, the consequence is a desire for reunion: when the union is fulfilling, a desire for further differentiation and separateness follows.

Psychologically it is the same: when the happening between two persons is played out properly, each separately and within himself unifies (integrates, remembers, realizes, synthesizes) a bit of himself, which, in turn, becomes his newly differentiated self in search of union. Whether we discuss you and me under the glorious and colossal title of *Totality and Infinity* as does Levinas,* or simply speak of you and me in the here and now, the fundamental and endless happening between us is the process of separating and unifying.

For the happening to function properly, separating must be done correctly. It can be neither an escape nor a retreat. Running away from home, for example, is an improper separation which promises trouble in the next union. The alternative is not necessarily to stay. The alternative is to walk away, not run; to shout and cry the anguish of the union and perhaps the fear in the leaving, too; and then, if the desire to go is still present, to leave. ·

When a phase of separating is completed properly, the state of separateness which follows is unencumbered by disturbing residuals. There is neither pride nor regret; contempt nor guilt. Excitement—sometimes felt as fear—characterizes the state of separateness as the desire for new union awakens and the search begins, now with new, and as yet untested, skills. There is a deep sense of very personal satisfaction in feeling one's own boundaries, relishing the uniqueness of one's own singular existence coupled with the perplexing, yet rather pleasant, sensation of having two centers, one private and one shared.

The unifying phase of the process also requires care and is characterized by a deeply personal mutuality—an exchange in kind. It is not the lopsided reciprocity of teacher and student, the entertainer and his audience or the therapist and his patient. Admiration, applause, submission and cash are consolation prizes for the absent mutuality. Nor is it onesided. Information, amusement and help are the consolation prizes given out by the teacher, the entertainer and the therapist, respectively, in lieu of person. At best, such connections provide encouragement and temporary relief from the discomfort of a jammed process of unifying and separating. Proper unification struggles stubbornly for corre-

* Levinas, Emmanuel, TOTALITY AND INFINITY, Duquesne University Press, Pittsburgh, Pennsylvania, USA, 1969.

spondence when it is needed, yet refuses it should it be given grudgingly. Similarly, it is a willingness to meet the other's need—whether for unity or separateness—but only if it can be done whole-heartedly. Otherwise, it prefers a forthright disclosure of differences and takes the risk of a fight, if necessary, in order to protect the sanctity of the union. Proper unification is a dedication not to the other but rather to life as it is lived with the other.

Fulfillment and a remarkable sense of limitlessness characterize the successful union. At best, one feels that now all is possible; at worst, that life is bearable. There is an important distinction between being filled and fulfilled. Students are filled; lovers are fulfilled. Filling depends largely on the other while fulfillment rests more in one's own hands, having to do with knowing what one wants, seeking it from the other with a full head of steam and grieving properly if it doesn't come. Fulfillment is a realization that leads to new separateness: a separateness which may root the union more solidly in the reality of what is available; or, a separateness that directs one to seek the needed unity elsewhere. Family therapists do not prescribe partners; they only oil the process of separating and unifying.

5. THE ESSENTIAL INGREDIENTS

As exemplified in the union of the newly born infant and its full-breasted mother, the simplest form of the ever spiralling process of unifying and separating begins with desire which is fulfilled and concluded by a state of calm awaiting the next desire. Thus, the fundamental ingredients are desire—fulfillment—calm.

The process is rarely so simple. Often, desires do not match. Then, conflict and struggle must be added as necessary steps in the process which is now characterized by desire—conflict—struggle—fulfillment—calm.

For example, a father reads his child a bedtime story, fulfilling a desire in both of them for union. But, as sometimes happens, fulfillment does not parallel. When the story is finished, father is ready to leave—ready for separateness—while his daughter, not yet drowsy, would prefer continued union. Father says, "Goodnight", and daughter asks for a glass of water. As both press for what they each want the conflict breaks out into open struggling. Father yells, "Stop stalling!" while daughter cries, "I'm not. I really am thirsty—and a little hungry, too." The conflict and struggle provide both separateness (of position) and union (joined in struggle) and hopefully continues until relative calm is achieved for both. The conflict and struggle are essential ingredients.

Attempts to prematurely eliminate essential conflict from the spiral are common. "Let's not spoil a pleasant evening with a quarrel." But, it is often the quarrel, if pursued properly, that is the necessary icing which must be put on the cake of desire before one can taste the joy of completion, whether it be union or separation.

Struggle is to conflict what gastric juice is to digestion, yet, there are those who attempt to meet discord without struggle. They make contracts, deals, agreements and understandings. Sometimes, crude denial is also tried in the vain hope of stabilizing a shaky union. Such items do not stabilize, they paralyze. The result is secret struggle without relief, guerrilla fighting and a family member with a persistent symptom.

When the conflict and struggle are insufficient to complete the process, another ingredient must be introduced. Fulfillment is replaced by grief. Then, the path from desire to calm is: desire—conflict—struggle—grief—calm.

Grief is another essential ingredient which many try to exclude from the life process of separating and unifying. But, grief is to separating what contentment is to union—its natural consequence—and must be experienced, not exempted. When blocked, the separating aspects of the process become clouded by dread, while union is extolled and overvalued—or recklessly disdained. Security becomes a preoccupation and union is clutched nervously rather than welcomed with an open hand.

Nothing is forever. It is possible to separate and rejoin without conflict, struggle and grief, just as it is possible to love thy neighbor as thyself. But such coveted activities are not beginning points, they are end results. Both are the consequence of struggling properly with others, as with oneself.

The healthy happening then, born of paradoxical desires for union and separation, searches eagerly, though sometimes painfully and filled with fear; and, when a phase is completed, rests calmly in preparation for its next activity, its next desire, its next seeking which it knows it must have. And it judges the success of its previous round by the changes that characterize the new happening, and not by the absence of conflict.

6. THERAPY: INFLUENCING THE HINDERED HAPPENING

Delightful desire, sparkling conflict and luxurious calm characterize the course of the healthy happening. When the process gets stuck, the happening becomes, instead, a continuous, dull, gray pain characterized by boredom and indifference, physical aches and pains, loneliness and depression, frustration and rage, bitterness and cynicism—and chronic interpersonal discontent.

The stuck happening has four features, reminiscent of Man's most primitive thoughts about himself in the universe.

There are always two elements in conflict

> me vs you
> me vs my headache
> me vs my impotence
> me vs my ideals

One is always the oppressor of the other, the victim

> My head hurts me.
> You frustrate me.

> You are too good for me.
> You overwhelm me.

The victim is always me

The victim is always innocent

> I wish I could influence (you, my headache, your over-
> whelming, my impotence, the Gods), but I don't know how.
> Maybe, if I sacrifice . . .

The task of therapy is to arouse (remind) forgotten desires; to fire
up abandoned conflict; and to keep all combatants at the front
until everyone wins. In the wake of such victories, new and old
struggles will awaken and be guided similarly. When the family
catches on to the therapeutic process, therapy is ended.

Selecting The Working Point

Resolving a petty, commonplace everyday and current conflict is
the reference point for all therapeutic activity (until resolved or
replaced by another immediate conflict of a higher order, i.e., one
that encompasses it). With that in mind, the therapist continually
locates his working point by processing. Regardless of the number
of family members and irrespective of the many things happening
at once, the therapist, with himself as the starting point, selects as
the other point the greatest obstacle to resolving that current conflict, and engages it. (If he can't find it, his own lostness becomes
the other point for a brief engagement, either alone or with the
help of the family.)

> The therapist's eye and a father's scowl engage. Father says
> it's for his daughter, Jan. The scowl and Jan are introduced.
> Their conversation grates painfully. The therapist's discontent
> and the mother's restlessness momentarily engage and are freed
> by the therapist's invitation for Mother to speak. She tells
> Father that he is unfair: that Jan is not as bad as he implies.
> Mother and Father become the new working point as they
> heatedly debate Jan's ultimate goodness. Before the therapist

70

can disrupt the senseless bickering, Jan's brother, Rick, comes in on Father's side. Jan attacks Rick. Father attacks Jan for attacking Rick. Mother soberly points out Father's behavior as further evidence of unfairness towards Jan. The therapist is now content: the family is conversing.

As the melee continues, Father becomes loud and abusive towards Mother, accusing her, among other things, of collusion with Jan to victimize him. Mother effectively neutralizes his anger with tears and, as frequently seen in many homes, by so doing also stops the discussion. The therapist's desire for resolution silently objects to the cease fire. He doesn't know which way to press so he engages himself for a moment of internal dialogue. He sees the children as healthy, loyal, vigorous and innocent pawns. He thinks Mother is right but Father succumbs to her tears rather than to her wisdom. The therapist must leave his reverie to face Father. Which shall it be, content or process? Support Mother's wisdom or confront Father's giving in to tears? The therapist's inner search leads him elsewhere and he must follow: Father's overabundant anger is seen as the greatest obstacle. It tarnishes every family conversation. The therapist's desire for resolution and the father's anger become the engaged points as the therapist says to Father: Your anger is your enemy, not your wife. It blinds you from seeing your family. It leaps into every conversation like a young pup. But I think it's an old dog and I want to know it better. What's the greatest frustration of your entire life?

The therapist does not expect a ready answer, but the search for the real target of Father's anger is the now working point for the entire family. It is a necessary side trip, perhaps a visit to some ancient ruins, but a tour for the whole family to take with him. Hopefully, they will all return better equipped to resolve the current conflict in which Father's frustration was aroused.

Conversation Is The Medium
Not only is conversation the vehicle through which the treatment is mediated, but it is through conversation that the most refined understanding and the most exquisite communion can be achieved.

71

More than that: it is through language and the spoken word that man can change himself.

But not all conversation brings beneficial changes. Conversation designed to mask the speaker, to manipulate the other, to avoid the personal meeting, is not likely to bring with it intimacy or change. Therapeutic conversation—those conversations which lead towards intimacy and enhance the possibilities for personal development—are expressive, revealing, self-disclosing. Words of others can guide; can provide understanding; can bring new perspectives; can inspire or discourage; but, it is only the words that come out of one's own mouth, and, by their very expression, that one changes (or, in terms of therapy, that one is cured).

In a very real sense then, the therapist is not therapeutic. At best, he can be therapeutic-enhancing: he can only guide family members towards the therapeutic words each must speak for himself.

THE THERAPEUTIC MECHANISM

For a remark to be therapeutic, i.e., to change the speaker, four conditions must be met.

1. *There must be struggle*
Change is forged in the fires of struggle. Casual conversation provides knowledge and understanding and, at best, can bring one into a conflict zone. But before there can be change there must be struggle: and, before there can be struggle there must be discord. Struggle need not always be deadly. It can be exciting, refreshing, challenging and even joyful. But it requires sweat and tears. Struggle need not always be between two people: it is often with oneself. But it cannot be with inanimate objects or impersonal ideals. It must be personal.

2. *The other—the listener—must be significant*
Revealing one's deepest concerns to a relative stranger (friend,

therapist, priest, bartender) brings confessional relief, not change. Screaming one's anger to a frustrating motorist, likewise, accomplishes little. The disclosure must have as its object, a significant other, a person with whom one struggles for union and separateness, a person with whom one's life feels risked when one speaks. Even when the disclosure is an admission to oneself that needs only to be exteriorized, the significant other who simply serves as a witness to the testimony must be qualified. The witness could be a devoted pet, but it cannot be a fool or a stranger.

3. *The words must be the right words*
The message must be the deepest possible concerted summation of one's existence at that moment in that situation. It can be an elaborate plea or a simply expressed realization, such as, "I can't." It is the fullness of the message, and nothing more, which makes the words right. When the words are right there is no ambivalence, no uncertainty, no accusation, no self-recrimination. There is only realization with its attendant anguish.

4. *The words must ride on the crest of the corresponding affect*
Words, no matter how personal and regardless of their pertinence in the face of a significant other, fail when uttered through cold teeth. The affect (the music) is required for the message to be complete. By the same token, music, no matter how grand, cannot cure without words. Without words, there is only relief: without music there is only understanding.

"How do you feel?" is a common query of therapist's which tends to arouse answers, not affects. It is a foolish question. Feeling is aroused when one speaks the right words. If it isn't, then awareness of what one is really saying is the missing element.
Although the mind can benumb awareness, the body cannot. Verbal expression of body sensations and movements in that moment can more readily re-ignite awareness and unleash affects. The appropriate affect affirms the words and augurs change.

The mourning reaction provides a relatively pure example of the four essential ingredients. Change—in this instance release from the grief of permanent physical separation—comes when the words and music are delivered, in unison, directly to the deceased. Crying, shouting, hating, screaming and aching silently, are all parts of the necessary total work to be done. When done thoroughly each time (it often requires repetition over a period of years) there occur, finally, both a reconciled separateness and deeply realized union with the deceased—without burdensome residuals. The mementos can be put away.

When a family comes to therapy, the first two conditions are already provided: there is conflict and the presence of significant others. Initially, the therapist need only guide their conversing (3 and 4).

From time to time, more than guidance is needed. Inevitably, conflicts arise between the therapist and various family members, and then, he can no longer remain the dispassionate guide. He must bring himself to the struggle prepared to change. Otherwise, under a guise of professionalism, he will imply that he is always right and that only his patient need change.

To argue that the therapist's personal reactions belong exclusively to him is to warp the issue and damage precious potentials for his own growth. Where he first learned his reactions and why he developed them are both irrelevant issues. It is sufficient to know that everyone comes by his behavior honestly, i.e., because of the unique circumstances of his life, and to leave the matter there. The living issue is *now*. By starting with the premise that responses belong to the person who arouses them rather than to the one with whom they were initiated, the chance for a personal reaction is immediately introduced, and consequently, the possibility for new experience, awareness and growth.

Another may wonder, "How can I get that worked up? After all, this family member is not a significant other for me, and without that ingredient there is neither cause for such involvement nor benefit to be derived from it." But there are both cause and

74

benefits. It is not a question of whether the therapist can get "that" worked up. If he takes his work and his life time seriously, he will be aroused—and often. A more interesting question is what he does with his arousal. Does he gossip it to a spouse or colleague? Write an article? Take it to his own therapist?

By keeping his arousal in his work and directing it to the person who arouses it, the therapist brings reality to the therapy and authenticity to his relationships with the various family members. Additionally, his exemplary behavior sets the optimal tone for family conversations: an atmosphere of courageous self-disclosure. And, most importantly, for each family member towards whom he may from time to time direct his personal message he offers the chance to stand on equal ground and to feel significant. "How in the hell can you stand by and let your kids talk to your wife that way!" spoken with all the associated affect, is more beneficial for all, than a cool, "You seem blocked. I wonder what you are feeling just now?"—to be followed by a professional treatise entitled, *The Problem Of The Passive Father.*

Therapists would do well to take the following Oath: In the interests of myself and my patients, I will face everyone with whom I choose to share my time as a significant other, whether he likes it or not.

The procedure for poignant personal change is better known in religious circles than it is in the field of psychology. Perhaps this has to do with the fact that the significant other (God) does not confound the already difficult task with petty personality traits of his own. For instance, Job (7:11) speaks of his frustration with God by saying to Him,

> Therefore I will not refrain my mouth: I will speak the anguish of my spirit: I will complain in the bitterness of my soul.

The proverbial patience of Job is suspect. If he is to be considered a patient man, it is obviously an active, dynamic, working patience. He does not keep still. Repeatedly he expostulates with God as

75

he searches for comprehension beyond reason. Finally he is rewarded. His greater self (God) is revealed to him, his anguish leaves, and once again all are reminded of the path for change.

Admittedly, Job had it easier than most of us. His work was not complicated by an argumentative other. Also, Job had his own blameless behavior behind him and a complete faith in the other before him.

Although the task of finding one's own inner light through another human being is complicated by the clash of personalities and our own tarnished faith in both ourselves and the other, the path is still the same: persevering self-disclosure that protests and praises aloud.

7. THE FAMILY: SUSTAINING THE HAPPENING

Frequently one hears, "Well, in the last analysis, it is only oneself that one must face." And, with that thought, they plunge into the work that Perls so masterfully brought to the psychotherapeutic scene. They confront themselves at every turn, they allow themselves no respite. With a shrug and an, "Oh, well, it can't be helped," they love and forgive themselves when they cannot go further. They differentiate and integrate themselves. And, when it is all finished they stand erect, ready and eager, but with the disturbing question, "Now what?".

Had the same struggle been waged in the context of a greater struggle between two people, there would be less likelihood of the "Now what?" residual. This remnant suggests a premature circuit closure. It takes a long time—more time than most live—to get enough from others in the proper way so that one becomes sufficient unto oneself. To be so sufficient does not mean one no longer needs others. On the contrary. It means knowing the necessity for others, particularly when deficits in oneself are discovered. It means knowing how to use others as the necessary scaffolding while gaining the strength and the skill to restore oneself, and not to mistake others for building materials. It means knowing the eager, "Now what?", asks searchingly, "Now what do I yet need, and with whom?".

It is not enough to know something. Nor is it enough to do something. Knowledge develops ideas, not people. Action develops skills, it does not humanize. Before one can get beyond the elephant, one must see oneself. To achieve that one must be seen. Before one can get beyond the elephant, one must hear his own voice. To achieve that one must be heard. To reach one's highest potential, it is not enough to see one's own image in a lake, or to think one's own thoughts silently—or to shout them in the pristine forest. Youngsters know well that their knowings and doings are not enough, and they are innocent enough to tell someone without embarassment, and wise enough to speak without hesitation or cunning. (Today my young son Noah said, "Isn't it funny that we can't feel the blood and bones in our stomachs?" Hearing his own awareness as it passes through a listening other and returns to his own ear was the essential phenomenon. Getting an answer from me was inconsequential.) They know that the humanizing process comes literally through *re-lating*—through recounting oneself to another.

And they know more. They know that it can't be just anyone. They know it must be one who values their life as his own. Whether for child or adult, the therapist, no matter how skilled or personal, cannot go the full distance, cannot provide that level of significance. He can approximate it, he can give a taste, a hope, and, at best, a fragment of it when his own developing life crosses, for a brief moment, the developing life of his patient. But to sustain the process requires more than a fragmentary significant other. One must have an indwelling other, a person whose living is experienced as though it were a vital organ inside one's own body.

A path for continuing change (growth and repair) has been suggested earlier: to alter the natural procedure; to face whoever one meets as a potentially significant other. But this is a dedication to (one's own) life that few choose deliberately. For most, it is the reverse: the desire for a relationship with an already significant other (a family member, usually) is the needed force which motivates one to the task of changing.

That is understandable. The issue is fundamental change and not minor personality adjustments like learning not to be sarcastic. The union of which we speak is a dedication to life, not a joint bank account; and the separateness sought is not a willingness to stand alone, but an ability to stand apart, when necessary, while struggling for a union that better serves both. (Along the way, practical problems are met and social behavior will change though such relief alone is not the goal.)

Such changes are not easily achieved. One must go through the rigors of hell each revealing inch of the way, experiencing the loss of treasured traits and valued virtues as though it were death itself. There are no volunteers. Everyone who goes is forced, either by an already existing unbearable pain inside himself, or by family, i.e., a significant other with whom he cannot live and cannot live without. And, as a rule, without a family to inspire the task, unbearable pain within is dealt with largely by denial, desensitization and social achievement.

Essentially then, for most it is intimate adult relating, in short, family, that provides the necessary inspiration (and insurance) for continued growth. Adult, because it is too easy to be committed to one's own children and still hide. Children are often lifesaving, for instance, inspiring a depressed mother to hang on. But they are not likely to do more than that as they are too innocent, too willing to accept what is, too ready to explain their experienced deprivation as natural, or to find fault beyond the relatedness, often in themselves.

Also, reciprocity is an essential ingredient for continued growth. As the child grows, the relevance of the parent's chief life struggles and that of the child's diminishes. By contrast, the struggles of related adults contain the possibility of increasing relevance.

78

Family is more than inspiration. Without the indwelling other—
an adult whose life we measure as our own (love)—there is
the risk of becoming the victims of our own logical minds, living
lives guided, at best, by sensitive intelligence and practical reality.
Family is necessary to effectively assail the bastions of reason and
carry us beyond. For adults and children alike, family is essential
to sustaining, in the deepest sense, the happening we call living;
and without whom life is reduced to an intelligent reflex arc.

4

The Elements of personal conversation

Conversation comes in two models: commercial and personal.
Beginning at home, as parents dote with pride over baby's first
words (Mama, bottle, milk, toy, bed), commercial style conversation focuses on objects. School aggravates object orientation with
each so-called subject taught. Referring to the classroom topic of
the moment, the educational by-word is "pay attention!". Social
discourse follows the trend and becomes largely a discussion of
topics.

> Where did you get that lovely hat?
> The weather has been dreadful lately.
> Seen any good movies, lately?
> The world is going to Hell.
> They could have won the ballgame, if only . . .

Commerce adds the final touch and rewards a worker, in large
part, for his ability to focus exclusively (outside of himself) on the
work to be done or the product to be sold. Personal reaction is
discouraged unless it can be of commercial value, and then it is
carefully confined to the suggestion box in the corridor, or special
brainstorming meetings where personal reactions are permitted to
leak out in a controlled ecologically conscious atmosphere.

Personal conversation, although generally received with less
enthusiasm, also begins at home and, by contrast, reflects what is
going on inside the person. Its first word is "No!", soon followed
by an endless undulation between I want this: I don't want that.
Its object is the subject of itself and its battle with the commercial
model is generally a losing one.

The terms subject and object, subjective and objective have become tangled. The Commercial—Education—Social model refers to the topic under consideration equally as the subject or as the object, while to be subjective is to introduce personal opinion (and considered poor form) and to be objective is to be laudably without personal bias (the concept of the immaculate perception).

Personal conversation perceives matters differently. I am the subject and you, to whom I speak, are the object. If we should discuss something beyond you, me or our relatedness, it is best called a topic. In personal conversation, the terms subjective and objective are meaningless: there are only your reflections and mine. All is said to be subjective, and an objective truth merely signifies that our reflections are in agreement.

This chapter magnifies the elements of personal conversation. It also calls attention to common conversational forms which are either unnecessary in personal conversation or are potentially damaging. As with any magnified study, the elements loom larger than real. They are elaborated more as an exercise than a prescription. A person who converses personally is known by his piquancy more than by his deft usage of the elements for personal conversation.

1. THE BASIC ELEMENTS

The fundamental unit of personal conversation is the declarative statement. Its ingredients are a subject, a predicate and an object.

A. The first word is "I".

> Contrary to all formal education which urges a modesty none possess, personal conversation calls for the use of "I" at the beginning of all sentences.

I wish I could feel loved by you.   NOT You don't love me.
I need that so much.

I hate you when you tell me what to do.   NOT You always seem so bossy.

I don't want you to talk to me so crudely.   NOT Would you talk to your mother like that?

Beware: "I think that you . . ." is not an "I" statement.

B. The basic verbs are active, personal and transitive.

>   I want; I don't want: I will; I won't: I like; I dislike.

Words are a suppliment and never a substitute for concerted behavior. In personal conversation, action replaces "I am".

Affection	Replaces	I am in love.
Departure	Replaces	I am going.
Crying	Replaces	I am sad.
Shouting	Replaces	I am angry.

Verbs are to be used assertively, not defensively.

I want your interest: I don't like your pity.   NOT I don't want to seem unappreciative but

Whether implied or explicit, the tense is always present.

>   I have always needed more from you than I have gotten (is how deeply I feel about this matter just now).

>   I will love you forever (reveals the intensity of the immediate feeling and is neither a promise nor a prediction).

C. The object is the person to whom you are speaking. Personal conversation is disclosing some perspective, feeling, attitude, thought that each has about himself in relation to the other. Too often, a topic becomes the object instead of the person spoken to.

>   *She:* I feel so alone most of the time: like we aren't really married. I don't like it at all.

He: What should we do about it?

She is no longer the topic. "It"(the feeling) has become the topic. And the tense has changed to the future. The risk now is that the rest of the conservation will reduce to planning future activities. There is nothing wrong with planning, per se, but it is better when it is a treat rather than a treatment. The good feeling and the desire come first.

A more personal response to her pain, which would include a measure of immediate fulfillment, would be simply, "I want to hear more." And, if true, "I feel a bit as you do."

Or, if he were not resonating with her need; "I don't feel as you do. I'm quite satisfied with our marriage in this respect."

Or, "I'd like to be with you right now, but I don't want to talk about that."

Talking topics instead of talking to one another aggravates, if not generates, the commonplace sense of distance and isolation.

2. THE ROLE OF GOSSIP

Gossip is a leech that sucks the potential life out of the body of two personal conversations. It deprives an immediate encounter of its own necessary basic ingredients and it drains another possible conversation of needed energy, if indeed, it does not abort it completely. Direct remarks, haltingly spoken are preferable to easy references about someone else. In a phrase: talk to, not about.

Exceptions:
Talking something over with a third party in preparation for a face to face confrontation, converts debilitating gossip into profitable service.

For clarification purposes

> *Husband to wife:* I've got to tell my boss some things he isn't going to like and I don't know how to say it without getting fired. I'd like to sound it out with you awhile. O.K.?

To clear away excessive ebullience

> *Husband to wife* (about their 15 year old who has taken the family car without permission): I'll kill that kid when he gets home. I'll teach him a lesson. Who in hell does he think he is to treat us like this? Wait till I get my hands on him.

A wife, familiar with the dynamics of personal conversation and interested in protecting her son from overkill, would first pacify her husband by gently encouraging him to spew on rather than by trying to mollify him immediately.

Often it is necessary for parents to discuss matters of family welfare that involve the children. This search for concerted and responsible leadership could hardly be called gossip; though, as children get older, permitting children to share such discussion can both enrich the search and provide the children with valuable experiences in topical, yet personal conversation.

3. IS THE QUESTION NECESSARY?

The purpose of the question is to obtain information. Since personal conversation is essentially a matter of self-disclosure, the information sought lies within, and questions to others become largely superfluous. In personal conversation, questions are best converted into statements.

Questions can be dangerous, leading important conversations astray.

> Do you have another woman?

risks a defensive answer and an irrelevant argument.

> There's something missing for me in our relationship and I
> would like to talk with you about it.

This puts the conversation on course to begin the needed re-appraisal. Specifying the unfulfilled desires and inviting feedback propels personal conversation on its way.

Questions can stymie needed growth. During a family interview, a mother repeatedly asks her daughter, "What do you think of me?" The daughter tries various answers, generally reassuring, but to no avail. When the mother is urged to convert her question into a statement, the conversation went something like this: "I want you to think well of me, to assure me that I am a good mother. I live in constant fear that I am not. I have such terrible doubts as to what a good mother is. You see, I never had one." With this disclosure, the mother began to cry. She was encouraged to direct her further remarks, in fantasy, to her own mother, for whom they were so obviously meant and in this incounter (See Chapter 5) she began to complete the unfinished business that could never be achieved by asking her daughter, "What do you think of me?"

Questions are often a desire for engagement from a position of seeming bankruptcy—the asker simply has nothing to say. "What are you thinking about?", is a common probe of this type and is justifiably met with a querulous, "What's it to you?"

However, the problem is more a consequence of one's commercial orientation than a matter of valid emptiness. Searching for the statement may reveal one of the following:

> I have no topic to discuss but I would like to stir something up
> with you. (That, of course, is the topic.)

> I have things to say but I can't believe anyone is interested in
> them.

> I ask you questions because I envy you and look for flaws in
> your answers, but I dare not show you my envy. I'm afraid
> you'll discard me, if I do.

85

A husband, prepares to divorce his wife because of what he interprets as her constant accusations which come (as they easily can) in the form of questions. Where did you go? Why did you take a second cup of tea? What does this headline mean? Why are you driving down this street instead of taking the freeway? When unscrambled, for him questions were used as a standard form of criticism throughout his childhood and his allergy to them was enormous. His wife, on the other hand, used questions only as a form of engagement, a way of being seen by him, the only way she was ever able to get acknowledged by her father. Questions in personal conversation can never satisfy, since the answer lies buried in the asker, but personal conversation in which questions are thwarted can uncover that buried treasure—and spend it.

In two specific circumstances, questions in personal conversation can be beneficial.

1) When feedback is lacking

> What do you think of what I said?
> What's your reaction?

Or, simply,

> I'd like some feedback.

2) For clarification

> Starting with, "Do you mean" and adding your interpretation of what has been heard is better than a nondescript, and ambiguous, "What do you mean?", which also, could suggest disbelief (What do you mean by that?) or veil an attack (What do you mean by the foolish remark?).

Failure to hear leads to a statement, not a question,

> I didn't hear what you said.

possibly adding additional evidence of interest,

> Please say it again. I'd like to hear it.

86

Questions in personal conversation then, become merely a matter of individual style; and, as long as both parties realize that they are, in fact, statements, questions are harmless, often adding local color.

Are you serious?   FOR I find that incredible.

Do you think I'm a fool?   FOR I don't believe you.

Will you marry me? deserves the
answer, Are you serious?

4. THOUGHTS ON THINKING ALOUD

The presence of a qualified other as a sounding board or, perhaps, as a witness to a personal testimony may be all that is needed. When included in a personal conversation—an appropriate place for such activity—it is best declared in advance to avoid confusion or interruption.

> I need to think something through aloud. Could you just listen awhile? I don't really need your opinion, I just need to circulate through someone I respect.

During personal conversation, sentences often are merely such musings, and when not recognized, can make trouble. For instance, during an irritating, Why can't I—Because you just can't, debate with her 10 year old, a mother exclaims, "I don't know what ever possessed me to get married and have children." Usually familiarity is sufficient to provide the needed perspective for such musings, but should the mother notice a wince or should that remark succeed in stopping the child, it would be appropriate for the mother (or whoever else is present and picks up on it) to distinguish for the child, the difference between musings and messages.

Thinking aloud can innocently confound conversations between intimate adults, also. A husband and wife happily celebrate their tenth anniversary. Their conversation is a pleasant mixture of musings and messages until the husband muses,

I wonder why I ever decided to get married.

His wife hears it as a negative message, which often it is, and responds,

She: Now what's the matter? I thought things were so fine between us

He: They are.

She: They must not be if you have doubts about being married.

He: Haven't you ever wondered about that?

She: I wasn't having any doubts this evening.

He: Neither was I.

She: But, you said . . . .

He: I was just thinking how lucky I am. When I decided to marry I had no idea, really, what marriage was all about.

Thinking aloud, a valuable personal activity for many reasons, is a special dimension in personal conversations. Whether by advance declaration, intimate familiarity, or by further inquiry, the ability to distinguish mutters from missiles reduces the risk of needless detours in personal conversation.

5. THE DEPRIVING MODIFIERS

A host of qualifying words, phrases and attitudes, largely developed from the commercial model and designed to obscure or drug the personal elements, creep into personal conversations and drain them of essential vitality. They range from empty verbal tipping (thank you, excuse me but) to more subtle forms such as second guessing (not saying something on a hunch that the other might respond unfavorably, thus avoiding the possible unwanted reaction). A few of these manipulative devices are sampled here. They are too numerous to list.

A. *Preambles*

Preambles, commonly used in commercial conversations for the purpose of qualifying, are often misused in personal conversation to appear modest and unassuming (obscuring the subject: I). In personal talk they distract more than they disguise but, worse than either, they pale participation.

> I think that
>
> I feel that
>
> I think that I feel
>
> If you don't mind my saying so, it seems to me that the truth of the matter is that it would be best, under the circumstances, if I say nothing about

Stripping away preambles brings people up front and sparks conversation.

B. *Doubting*

Doubt, at first glance, may appear as a reasonable, if not downright admirable, element. Yet, in personal conversation, there is no such thing as doubt. Uncertainty is a posture, not a fact. In commercial conversation, when discussing a topic, there can be doubt, e.g., one may be uncertain about the distance to the moon. But, there is no personal uncertainty about that uncertainty. "I'm not sure," in personal conversation is a definite position from which, if true, the person will act. Doubt expressed about one's competence or personal qualification in a personal relationship is either an erroneous conviction or a frank deception. Take the remark, "I doubt that I can bring you the happiness you want and should get from a mate."

First of all, that is for the other to decide. Secondly, it is a remark about the future. Now, the question is, what is the person who makes such a remark trying to do? Is it a veiled goodbye? Is it an expression of insecurity seeking to manipulate reassurance? Or, is it an innocent and sincere attitude created by a commercially grounded way of thinking?

The answer is to be found in the mouth of the doubtful one by requesting a doubtless desire in the present tense. It may be "There isn't enough here for me. I want more than I get from you."

Doubtlessly, a good place to begin a personal confab.
Should there be mutual interest in the possibilities between them, specifics and feedback will guide their exploration.

Doubt is often inspired by the fear that anything once said is written forever. It helps to know that statements only reveal who we are in this moment. The saying itself may bring immediate revision. Personal conversation is a matter of integrity, not eternity.

Confronting Doubt
Regardless of its origins or motives, doubtful remarks are to be exchanged for firm positions. This is achieved by confronting it and inviting substitution. If that fails, the therapist and the family are to regard the doubt as a negotiating position and insist that the doubter take the consequences.

The procedure follows the principles elaborated in Chapter Two. The reference point is desire. Whatever the topic, the doubter is to make simple unqualified statements: I like this; I don't like tat. I agree with this; I disagree with that. I believe this; I don't believe that. I want this; I don't want that. Should the doubter refuse with, "But I am not sure about what I want" (a teasing answer of limited value: Are you sure about that?) the time has come for the doubter to live his doubting without surcease or manipulative benefit.

Example

In one family, a mother's doubt is the uncontested ruler of the household. Should the rest of the family desire to go on a picnic, she doubts that the weather will hold, she is uncertain about what to prepare, she is unsure when they should leave. Suggestions of others are met with further uncertainty until all interest is lost and the picnic cancelled. Should one of the children want to go out at night, Mother's doubts about the advisability of the enterprise prevent the going. In the name of consideration and respect (also often used to deprive encountering), Father urges the boys not to "worry Mother." It was not difficult for an outsider to see that her doubts were absent when she approved of the activity. But, it was not so easy for Mother to see it. Mother could not doubt her doubting.

Eventually, the other members of the family could. Mother was permitted to continue doubting while the rest of the family based decisions on more practical considerations. Her doubting now impotent, Mother reluctantly begins to abandon her old friend, doubt. Her first (welcomed) certainty, naturally, was her unqualified resentment towards her doubt slayer: the family therapist.

A popular conditional format is the sprinkling of sentences with words like maybe, perhaps, if and possibly. They usually mask disagreement in order to avoid conflict. They are to be stricken from (or, ignored in) personal conversation—unconditionally.

C. *There is no adequate substitute for I*

Time, circumstances, the situation, they, it, one, etc., have all been misused to diminish response-ability.

Clear your places.	NOT This situation where everyone leaves his dirty dishes
I don't want to help you with your homework tonight.	NOT Gee, I'm sorry, but I just don't have time.
I can't stand living in this pigsty another minute!	NOT What would the neighbors think if

6. A NOTE ON SILENCE

Silence, like love, is a consequence, a conclusion, a contentment that follows the necessary adjustment of intimate living. When the angry, the sad, the fearful elements are resolved, what remains is a personal love for an individual or a neutrality that is not indifference. It is the same with silence: contentment comes at the end of talking, of saying what must be said, whether it be to spouse or child, God or the devil, himself. Silence, prescribed or premature fills with demons that destroy the calm in the heart of silence.

Yet, there are times one can properly refuse to listen, when it is sound—the right sound—to tell someone to shut their damn mouths, to stop their incessant, inane or intolerable babbling; or to walk away if silence cannot be had. To say, "Shut up" is not a command. It is an emphatic wish and a declaration, a show of limit. Albeit clumsily and unkindly spoken, it says, "Shut up and talk to me."

And what about the one who needs to speak? Is he to be ignored? Victimized? Silenced? Not necessarily. If he heeds the other's cry, he can search for new words, words that more clearly speak the message of desire within him at that moment. Should he find them, the whole world would listen.

7. CLOSURE

There are two consummate endings to a personal conversation and neither of them is understanding. Both are experiences. One is joyful, the other is sad. One ends with an embrace; the other with a greater separateness. Yet, both are satisfying and both know contentment.

Example
Morgan gets angry when Laury comes home late from work. Laury explains the necessity, feels a bit guilty, and soon gets angry, also,

accusing Morgan of being an unfair male. As the feeling spends both become reasonable: Morgan admits he's unfair and promises to be more understanding while Laury promises she will avoid unnecessary late work as much as she can. An uneasy peace prevails. In therapy, Morgan is asked to describe to Laury in minute detail, what happens inside of him between the time he comes home and Laury's later arrival.

> *Morgan:* I get busy. I put my things away, see if there's anything to do around the house, turn on some music. Then,
>
> I sit down in a soft chair and relax.
>
> *Therapist:* And, then?
>
> *Morgen:* I look at my watch and begin to wonder when Laury will come home. I start feeling annoyed.
>
> *Therapist:* I'm interested in what happens after you relax and before you become annoyed.

Morgan has never stayed there very long. He thinks hard.

> *Morgan:* I shrink. I get smaller. The walls become gigantic slabs of silence and I'm paralyzed with loneliness and insignificance. (He begins to shiver as he forces himself to remain in a reality he usually skims through quickly.)

Laury listens with tearfilled eyes as Morgan reveals (and heals) himself.

> *Therapist:* Talk to Laury, now.
>
> *Morgan:* I can't bear this feeling. And, I can't tell it to you because I feel like such a baby. (Such social concerns often lid potfulls of precious personal paraphernalia that need sharing.) I start to get angry with myself but then I think if you were home, this would all be avoided.

The details of his explanation are dross; her empathic response, dressing. He is in the process of healing himself through his disclosure.

Nonetheless, for Laury, he is no longer an unreasonable and dangerous male. He is a man, her man, whom she now knows a bit better. As for Morgan, there will be less fuel with which to fire up angry assaults on Laury when she comes home after he arrives.

Laury moves into his lap. Now, more as his woman than his salvation, Morgan can enjoy her a bit better, too.

The other closure, equally essential but far less popular, is the closure of separation. Growth depends on an unending oscillation between the two closures. Mistakenly, many idealize the closure of union (. . . and they lived happily ever after.) and spurn the closure of separation (Who wants to live in lonely isolation all his life!). Of course, both notions are as absurd as they are undesirable. Union no more portends continued happiness than separation means loneliness and isolation. Sporadic contentment (continuous joy is beyond consideration) comes from a healthy flowing between union and separation, while loneliness and isolation occur in both when there is no movement.

Separation is painful even when desired. Not because it promises isolation, but simply because it comes from a union. Were the union insignificant from the beginning, it is only a matter of movement, a departure, like a fly leaving the wall. But a child leaving home, a marriage breaking up, or just leaving after breakfast for a day's work is a different matter. A union—successful or not—is being broken and there must be pain. When ignored, the closure of separation is being treated too casually, and subsequent unions will be skimpier and stickier.

> Let's just say we disagree and let it go at that.

portends trouble. Although, at times, unavoidable, blurring differences by agreement as a form of closure only postpone a day of reckoning.

> To hell with you! Goodbye!

94

is a greeting, not a closure. It means there is work to be done. It is an excellent beginning. It immediately begins the work of clearing away blinding emotional debris, and is to be continued until the specifics can be spoken.

The only "good" bye is the one that has dispatched all of the attendant regret and remorse before the separation, leaving no residuals. Bitterness, resentment, pride, defiance, chagrin, feeling superior, accusation and self-recrimination are some of the signals of improper separation. They tell us one has opened what he thought was the front door and walked into a closet.

The closure of separation acknowledges the pain of separation as it simultaneously tastes the glory of separateness.

7

5

The Therapist intervenes

Once the initial amenities are completed, any utterances by the therapist can be seen as the consequence of his own inner discontent. When the interview is proceeding according to his expectations, the therapist is silent.

The therapist's interventions serve a dual purpose: to guide the family's negotiations and to relieve his own inner discomfort. As long as his comments also restore his equanimity, the therapist functions essentially as an impersonal guide. When, however, his neutral remarks are insufficient to relieve his inner unrest, he additionally and specifically includes his more personal reaction. Personal participation continues until relative detachment is restored.

Both purposes are inextricably interwoven and form the fabric of the therapist's intervening life. Here, for descriptive simplicity only, the therapist's interventions are divided into two categories: his essentially exclusive behavior as a guide, and his participation to relieve the balance of his personal reaction. Either aspect of the therapist's behavior can be beneficial or disruptive to the therapy, and the division bears no implications on that issue. The therapist's most beneficial influence is more a consequence of his ability to integrate the two functions than his talent for doing either one of them well.

1. THE GUIDING INTERVENTION

Guiding the interview consists of bringing family members to face each other squarely on whatever issues they may choose; to help them to meet one another in full strength; and to keep them on course until the issue is either resolved or superceded by an issue of greater moment. Guidance has two challenges: from the myriad of things happening, how does the therapist select his most suitable working point; and, when he does find it, how does he shape his intervention to get the optimal impact.

There are, of course, no absolutes. The most suitable working point is the point most suitable for each therapist; the optimal intervention, the one that best fits his personality. The topic here is how each therapist might find *his* best intervention, not *the* best one.

The following annotated transcript includes a personal account of the therapist's inner workings to expose the process through which one may locate his own guiding intervention. Suggestion: Scan the dialogue completely first; and then, re-read the transcript, this time including the detailed commentary.

Tina, age 16, the oldest of three children, ran away from home. Her parents locate her through girl friends, insist that she return home, and consult a family therapist. The initial interview opens with Tina's father announcing the difficulty diffusely, "We have a serious communication problem." When pressed for specifics, he becomes more general, saying, "Nobody can talk to anybody about anything." I think to myself, 'there's one problem right there', but decide it is too early to focus down on Father's movement towards greater vagueness when pressed for specifics. Instead, I turn to Mother.

> *Mother* (nodding towards Tina and Father): They argue all the time.
>
> *Hoping to initiate a family conversation, I redirect Mother's remark to them.*
>
> *Therapist:* What do the two of you have to say about that?

97

Father (answering to the therapist): It's true. We do argue a lot. But I don't know how to avoid it. There are certain things that must get done and she gives me a hard time about them. *Still preferring to be more instructive than penetrating, I make a mental note of Father's blameless, innocent attitude.*

Therapist: When you don't know what to do, consult your family. That's what families are for.

Common sense is the therapist's constant ally.

Although Father and Tina appear to be the two principles in this struggle, the topic (things to be done at home) could involve Mother. Therefore, I purposely do not suggest specifically that Father consult Tina (or Mother). By leaving that option to Father, I can learn something about the vectors in this family.

Father (turning to Tina): What is there to say? There are things to be done. I don't think I'm unreasonable about them.

Tina: You are always picking on me about something.

Father: Do what's necessary, and I wont need to remind you.

Tina does not answer, and the conversation stops.

Therapist (to Tina): I think conversations should be finished, not abandoned.

Tina (With an air of defiant hopelessness): What's the use? He wont listen.

Therapist: Then I suggest you settle that with him first.

Tina thinks about it a minute or two, by-passes the exact suggestion, but takes heart from my interest and returns to the struggle.

Tina (to Father): I do what's necessary. I do the shopping. I clean up. I take care of the kids.

Father: The sink is always full of dirty dishes, you fight with the other kids constantly, you . . .

Tina (interrupting): I'm not fighting with them. I'm just trying to keep them from making such a mess.

Father: Remember in the kitchen last week when you were hitting Marcy (Tina's 12 year old sister)? She wasn't making a mess. In fact, she was only trying to help you put the groceries away. (Turning to Marcy). Isn't that true?

Marcy nods.

Tina: I had just finished the shopping, and was putting the groceries away, myself. I didn't need help with that. I asked her to set the table for dinner and she wouldn't. She just kept pestering me.

Father: Hitting her is no way to solve anything. Maybe you could have set the table and let her put the groceries up. You were yelling at Paul (Age 10), also. He wasn't doing anything.

Tina (her voice becoming sad): He was messing up the front room and I had just cleaned it up before I went shopping.

Father: You could try to talk to him. You didn't have to yell at him and threaten him.

Tina gives up, again. Hope gone, she falls into a sad silence.

Generally, the preferred target for the guiding intervention is the process—*how* people talk to (or avoid) each other, while the content—what they say—is used more to guide the therapist in the selection of his process-directed intervention. However, when the therapist loses his neutrality, his personal values and prejudices are shared, and he speaks to content.

The therapist weighs process.

> *I think she made a good try. I see her as basically sound even though she cannot sustain her side of the struggle. After all, where can she learn how to struggle effectively. Mother doesn't seem to be much help and Father has lined up with the other kids against Tina At least she is close to her grief when she gives up. That's better than bitterness or resignation.*

99

The therapist weighs content.

It sounds like she's doing a lot around the house; perhaps not like an experienced mother, but she's certainly participating actively. Maybe, too actively. Father's frustration doesn't seem justified. There must be more to it than he has come up with so far. The concrete issues add up in favor of Tina and do not adequately explain Father's irritability nor justify his obvious partiality.
I don't want to get caught up in a debate with Father about his attitude. I think it would be better to see if I can get to the fire underneath it, to whatever is really causing it. Because of my initial experience with him (his going to the more general when I seek the specifics), I know that it would be pointless to ask him directly for the specifics of his frustration. It is better to go to the process, to what he is doing and see if calling attention to his attitude is more profitable. Meanwhile, I don't want Tina to feel that it's all his job and also, I want her to learn how to negotiate better, so I address both of them.

Therapist (to Father): You accuse your daughter with such vigor, you don't seem to notice or respond to her sadness. (And to Tina) Tina, I'm sure your sadness has something important to say, yet you are silent.

Father: I notice her sadness. It bothers me. I don't mean to attack her. I'm just so frustrated about all of this.

Therapist: Try talking about your frustrations, instead.

Father: I thought that's what I was doing.

Therapist (trying to dig deeper, but without much hope): It seems there is more to your frustration than what I've heard so far.

Father: Of course, there are always many frustrations everywhere, but I thought we were trying to solve this one first. It's a big one.

Again, when invited to be more specific, Father becomes more general. I abandon this attempt and decide to rev up the conversational motor again and listen for other discordant noises.

Therapist: I agree. It's a big one. Go on.

Father: I don't know what to tell you, Tina. I don't want to be unfair, but you know your Mother is not well, and I can't stay home from work. I don't know what else to do.

Tina: But you blame me for everything. The only time you ever talk to me is to criticize me for something.

Father: I'm only making suggestions to try to help.

I hear something important: Tina has revealed a desire. She asks, albeit backhandedly, for his positive attention—for his affection. Until now she has been only on the defensive and although I was looking for the desires of both of them, I was concentrating more on Father, since his behavior seemed to be more obstructive. Also, why help Tina to find and to bring her wishes to a man who sees her as his enemy? But now she does it spontaneously. The least I can do is acknowledge her desire. But I try for more. I'd like Father to respond to it, also. After all, he is a significant other for her. I can only acknowledge her desire and give her hope: he could acknowledge her and give her life.

Therapist (to Father): I heard her ask for something positive from you. Did you hear it?

Father: No. (Turning to Tina) What did you say?

Tina: You don't talk to me except to criticize me.

Father thinks hard awhile, probably searching for evidence with which to counter.

Father (no longer accusing, but still irritable): I never thought about that before, Tina. I guess I don't ever compliment you much. I'm too preoccupied with what still always needs to get done.

Tina (no longer sad or silent): Everything gets done: the things that really need to, anyway.

101

Father (trying to be more reasonable): Well, I'm not so sure about that. We still haven't solved the basic problem of getting things running smoothly.

Even though I don't trust his reasonableness to be deeply rooted (he's too frustrated yet to be truly reasonable), his need to try to be reasonable is forcing him downstream. Now the problem is not just Tina's behavior, but getting things running smoothly. This brings us nearer to the possibility of finding the real source of his frustration. Since frustration always masks desire, once his frustration is specified, we can discover the desire and its target.

Tina: Maybe if you didn't worry about everything so much.

By his touch of reasonableness, Tina readily changes from foe to supportive friend, evidencing her eagerness to co-operate.

Father (more sincerely reasonable): I know you try, Tina. (Then, not knowing where to turn, he regresses a bit) I don't want to start criticizing you again, but things just don't always get done. At least, not to my satisfaction.

His accusing posture is changing: he even considers his own standards as a factor, whereas earlier, they were beyond mentioning. But, now, there is silence. Tina apparently doesn't know what else to suggest and Father is stuck, also. I'm wondering if I'm the only one thinking that Father's frustration may have more to do with his wife's non-participation at home than with Tina's inadequate participation. I could get fancy and make all kinds of psychological interpretations about what is going on. It was my education and it flashes through me now. I think of Father's and Tina's struggle, which excludes Mother, as Oedipal in origin and I could use that to explain why neither thinks to invite Mother's participation at home, or here, during the interview. But I have found such meanderings diversionary, so instead I move in to the more immediate and practical aspect of Mother's defection.

I direct my intervention to Father. I could simply invite Mother, but then I would not learn what stops the others from doing it, nor would they get the chance to experience the task for themselves. Experience is the essential ingredient in this

therapy and I must not usurp it, if avoidable. (Were I over-
whelmed and compelled to call Mother in, I would have.)
Nor do I turn to Tina. It is Father's relationship to Mother
that is the largest missing ingredient in this struggle. I believe
the interparental relationship should be the most influential
one in the family and I try to keep it that way. Children are
treasured visitors in a home created by the parents.

Therapist (as neutrally as possible): You seem to turn to Tina
for everything, as though you expect nothing from your wife.

Father: She's been sick a lot. She can't do much around the
house.

I believe sickness, including most protracted physical disability,
is a common, self-inflicted life style for people who are un-
happy. His remark only tells me that she (therefore he, too)
does not get what she needs from their marriage. But I think
it foolish to bring that viewpoint in at this time. I don't believe
he could use it and it could therefore only lead to a discussion
about it. Since the same thing happens in the therapy session as
happens at home (it always *does), I prefer to focus on him*
bypassing her in the immediate situation.

The immediate is always the preferred arena.

Therapist: Are you saying that she is too ill to participate in
this discussion?

Father: No, of course not. I guess it's just that we are so used
to settling things without her.

Tina: She can't help it if she's sick.

I like Tina's remark and I don't like it. There seems to be a
loyalty in it which attempts to be protective of Mother, but,
also, I'm suspicious about a possible collusion with Father to
displace Mother.

Children inately move to fill in spaces in a family. If, for instance,
this father were to die tomorrow, Tina, or one of the other
children, gender irrelevant, would try to serve in his place. This

phenomenon transcends sexual considerations such as Oedipal and Electra concepts, probably rendering them fiction.

> *I hold Mother's withdrawal equally responsible in this situation. A bad scene always has everyones cooperation. No one is innocent. I just haven't gotten around to Mother, yet. I really want her to come in voluntarily or Father to bring her in. Now, I'm curious about who will make the next move. Father towards Mother? Father against Daughter? Mother towards the family? It could indicate where the greatest motivation is for restoration.*
>
> *I need all of the help I can get. But, instead of allies, I get silence. So, I proceed to clear my own troubled mind.*

Therapist (to Tina and Father): I have the notion that you two would prefer that Mother stay out.

Father: Not at all. As I've said, it's just habit.

Therapist: I don't see any motivation in you to break that habit. You seem helpless.

Father (smiling): I feel that way with her most of the time. What can I do?

> *I don't believe his question was serious, but I treat it seriously anyway, in order to press him further.*

Therapist: You can stop smiling and invite her to participate here, if that is your desire.

Father (soberly): Sure, I want her to. But, isn't that up to her?

Therapist: Don't your wishes count for anything?

Father: Well, it's hard to impose on her when she already is having such a hard time.

> *I don't know if he means what he is saying. Perhaps there are other, more significant factors that prevent him from engaging with his wife, but I think it best to find out by taking his words at face value and see what happens. Since I don't want to leave room for evasion, I say it with conviction. Then, he must either act on it or refuse. That would tend to flush out any other factors.*

Interventions are, also, experiments from which the therapist learns.

> *Therapist:* Impose on her. It's better than ignoring her.
>
> *Father* (after a thoughtful moment, turns to his wife): Seems like we've gotten into some bad habits, doesn't it?
>
> *She nods.*

As long as converation is on the move, it need not be interrupted to point up poor style (such as this father's vague questioning rather than stating his desire more directly).

> *Father:* What do you think we can do about it?
>
> *Mother* (seriously thoughtful): I really don't know. My life just feels so dead. I can't seem to get interested in anything.
>
> *Father:* It seems like it began right after your mother died. That's been a couple of years, now. Before that, you were o.k.
>
> *Tears come to Mother's eyes and I know immediately that her husband has revealed our next task: to create an incounter, a dialogue between the two mothers, so that Tina's mother can, through a proper grief reaction, leave her Mother's grave and return to her family. Tina, as all runaway children, was not the first to leave the family.*

INCOUNTERING

An incounter is a device for creating the needed conversation for change when there is no available other. It is a dialogue of one, a talking aloud in a witnessed and supervised setting to a very real though invisible other. It differs from thinking aloud, which is a soliloquy, a talking to oneself, a sounding of one's own voice to gain the perspective that comes from hearing one's own thoughts. An incounter is a genuine dialogue. There are two distinct parts and they negotiate with each other just as in any other vigorously contested encounter, with the singular exception that both parts are spoken by the same person.

The incounter is not a substitute for an encounter, which is always to be preferred. But sometimes an actual conversation is not possible for any number of reasons: the other may be found in a dream sequence; it may be a deceased relative; a memory; a treasured pet; a fantasy; a pain; a bit of one's own body; or, simply and directly, oneself. An incounter is the updated substitute for the story, the history, the recounting. In place of talking about then and there in the here and now, it establishes a there and now as the working arena.

It is a useful device, and when used properly it can catapult one into crisis and resolution far more quickly and thoroughly than the old system of telling it to the therapist (or, the barkeeper) over and over until finally decathected, or buried alive from sheer boredom.

Not all people have sufficient imagination or liberty to abandon familiar reality and talk to their own creation, which is, of course, as real as actual flesh, but of a different order. For those who have difficulty, there are gimmicks that can help. For example, Tina's Mother could have such difficulty talking to her dead mother.

> *Therapist:* I can see by your tears that you are still at your Mother's dying. Talk to her.
>
> *Mother:* I can't. She's not here.
>
> *Therapist:* In a sense, she is very much here—and everywhere you go, isn't she?
>
> *Mother:* Well, yes.
>
> *Therapist:* Where do you see her?
>
> *Mother* (crying increases): In the casket.
>
> *Therapist:* Stand alongside of it and talk to her.
>
> *Mother:* But she's dead.
>
> *Therapist:* Talk to her about that.

Intensifying the work can be done in many ways. As in common conversation, specifics are most useful. For instance, Tina's mother might be propelled by suggesting that she reveal the most painful or seemingly petty details of the dying scenes—a smell, a curtain, the lighting, a glance. Or, perhaps, by urging her to say the most difficult thing she could think of to tell her mother.

When the pain is imminent, yet the person is unable to project himself into an incounter, recounting is better than stopping. During the recounting, however, the therapist can continue to lead towards the incounter by, in this instance, for example, keeping the dead mother present.

> *Tina's mother:* My mother was such a good person.

> *Therapist:* I'm sure she is pleased to hear that. Go on.

Guiding an incounter is precisely the same as guiding any other conversation: the desires of each are sought, the specific messages clearly and thoroughly delivered.

Role Playing

Should the in-conversation stymie and should the therapist identify confidently with the lagging part, he may role play it to provide a supporting backdrop for further work.

Example

In another family, for example, during an argument with his wife, a husband blurts out, "You remind me of my father. You're here but you're not really here. It happens all the time." The therapist, seeing that the wife has been very much "here" believes the husband's perception of his wife is overcast by the shadow of his deceased father and suggests to the husband that he talk directly with his father. The husband tries.

> *Husband* (to his father): It's hard to contact you; to see you clearly. I can see you reading the newspaper in your big chair while I sit at your feet hoping you'll say something to me. It's always like this. (Then, after a searching pause) I really don't know what else to say. (He becomes silent.)

The husband's voice trembles, but, as he himself admits, he has difficulty engaging. Actually, he doesn't yet talk to his father. He only describes the scene *as if* he were there. But his discomfort says he is close.

> *Therapist:* Talk *to* him, if you can.
>
> *Husband* (with obvious distress): What can I say? How can I talk to someone who isn't there, who obviously isn't interested. (Silence again.)
>
> *Therapist-now-father:* I'm here now, and I want to hear you.
>
> *Husband-now-son:* I doubt it. All I have to say are terrible things.
>
> *Therapist-now-father:* I still want to hear them.
>
> *Husband-now-son* (beginning to squirm in his chair): Do you know I hate you? Do you know I feel contempt for you? Do you know sometimes I've wished I had another father, a *real* father, a ... (his sobbing blocks his speaking further).

As his sadness subsides, he remains silent.

> *Therapist-now-father:* I want to here more.
>
> *Husband-now-son:* I want to hear something You *never* say anything.
>
> *Therapist-now-father:* I feel pain, pain I had forgotten, pain just like yours—of living with a father who also was locked inside and couldn't talk to me. I am sorry for the pain I bring you, too. And I am grateful to you for helping me to remember.
>
> *Husband-now-son:* You know, strange as it may sound, I never thought of you like that. You were only my depriver. I couldn't see you, really. Just as you couldn't see me. (He begins crying again.) How can it end? I'm probably doing the same to my kids. How awful! How awful! Does it never end?

The therapist knows that it is ending; that the very process of feeling and revealing his pain to his father will alter his behavior towards his own son, and in this instance, towards his wife, also. Sometimes, such work embroils the therapist. Then, it is appropriate for the therapist to continue with a bit of his own work, either talking directly to his own father, or son; or perhaps, only saying something, through his own crying, about himself. Here, the therapist only needed to enjoy a few of his own tears as the incounter climaxed.

At the completion of an incountering episode, if not spontaneously forthcoming, an invitation is extended to revisit the scene that initiated the incounter. In this instance, when the husband finished his crying, he spontaneously looked at his wife and said,

> I can see how I come to you as I came to him. I wait for you to give me your attention while I burn inside. Now, I wonder if you are more available than I have realized.

Since part of the task is to separate and distinguish remembered relatives from present ones, it is generally inadvisable to use immediate family members (such as a spouse) to role play. The contamination from both sides tends to muddle more than to advance the job at hand.

Modified Incountering
Modified incountering is often quite helpful. It calls forth an unspoken element to be added to an encounter.

Example
A husband and wife are soberly discussing a possible separation. As they talk about its possible harmful effects on the children, the wife strokes her own hair with her left hand while her right is tightly clenched in her lap.

> *Therapist* (to wife): I'd like you to become aware of your hands and what they are doing, but don't stop them. Put a tongue on each and let them speak: your left hand to your hair first.

Wife: It says, "You are lonely, and need my comfort."

Therapist: Now speak the right hand to your husband but omit the preamble 'it says'. Speak your hand.

Wife (bursting into tears): I won't let you go!

A word of caution: sometimes, a would be incounterer wanting to please the therapist and yet unable to project himself, tries to fake it. The pretense must not be permitted to idle along. Suggest measures for facilitating (close your eyes, look at someone, first describe the scene); focus on the need to please the therapist at all costs; or, simply abandon this path entirely. Should the therapist be frustrated that his precious gimmick doesn't function properly, that outspoken message could serve as a relevant transition.

2. THE PERSONAL TOUCH

Simple guidance continues only as long as the therapist's equanimity is substantially restored during each sequence, leaving no residuals which would diminish or adversely distort his participation.

Disturbing residuals may be positive, such as a feeling of affection, empathy or sympathy, bringing with it, for instance, an ill-advised charity. Impeding residuals may be negative, such as a feeling of anger, resentment, contempt or disgust, and influence the therapist to avoid someone, to side injudiciously, or to become overprotective. Impeding residuals can be neutral, such as an embarrassment about not knowing how to manage in a situation causing the therapist to become unduly professional and distant.

Disturbed feelings are not the only manifestation of problematic residuals. There are, also, seemingly innocent thoughts (What's a fine fellow like him doing with a fishwife like her?), condemning conclusions (He is hopeless.), and professional diagnoses (Hmmmm. A textbook case of Paranoia.).

When the therapist is uncertain whether a residual is impeding his work, he can be certain that, at best, his uncertainty is an impedence. Exploring his uncertaintly aloud may dispel it.

> *Therapist* (to husband): As I listen to you my dislike for you grows, and I'm concerned that it may get in the way of my ability to help. (Then, to the specifics.) Despite my frequent reminders, whenever someone in your family tells you what he or she wants, you answer with explanations and promises. Promises are for politicians and explanations are for lovers. I wish you'd either tell them that you want to meet their demands and simply cannot, or that you flat out don't want to, and wont. (Invite feedback) I'd like a direct reaction to me now and not another explanation or promise to try harder.

A to-and-fro personal exchange is carried on until such time as the therapist's relative detachment is restored. Then, he returns to his position as guide, perhaps helping others present to express their reactions to his behavior, which they may consider unorthodox or unprofessional. The therapist, in keeping with the principles for personal conversation, would not, of course, argue that point; he would merely encourage their full concerted reaction.

In spite of what many therapists (and family members) fear, hiding the message is a greater hazard than the message.

Not all disturbances within the therapist arise as a consequence of what is happening in the therapy, itself. Sometimes, the therapist is distressed before the family arrives (See Chapter 2 section 2): sometimes, by something in the arrival, per se. Regardless of when or why, distracting influences are to be dealt with promptly and directly.

Example
On a first visit, the therapist is jolted by a severe, disfiguring scar on the face of the mother which makes him wince.

> *Therapist:* That's really quite a scar you've got there. Makes me wince. I feel like asking you all sorts of questions about it,

like how you got it, does it bother you, can something be done about it. But I know that's just my usual way of walking around my discomfort. It wouldn't be fair. I'm the one who needs to talk about this just now, not you. I immediately feel sympathy towards you and probably will be a bit easier with you (saying it diminishes the risk). I hope not. We'll see. I'd like to know if it bothers you when I talk to you so directly about your scar. I'm sure few would greet you as bluntly as I do.

Give specifics: ask for feedback. Give specifics: ask for feedback.

> *Mother:* It's a little embarassing.
>
> *Therapist:* I'm sorry for that. I would guess that many have the same reaction as I have, yet don't say anything.
>
> *Mother:* Oh, I'm sure of that!
>
> *Therapist:* I think it's better to flush reactions like mine out in the open immediately. For me it relieves some tension about it.
>
> *Mother:* I feel better about it now, too. I often don't know whether people are being kind to me just because of it.

The peak of the therapist's distress is gone. The receding residual keeps him on the subject as he simultaneously begins to move in the direction of starting a family conversation.

> *Therapist:* How about with your family: do you ever suspect them of pity?
>
> *Mother* (hesitantly): No . . . not really.
>
> *Therapist:* The way that you say it sounds like, 'Yes. Sometimes'.
>
> *Mother:* That's true. But it isn't often.
>
> *Therapist:* Often enough to make trouble?
>
> *Mother:* I don't believe so. At least, not any longer.

Therapist (to father): I'm wondering if you agree with her.

Conversation is maintained on the topic until the therapist is satisfied that the issue has been neutralized for all or until superceded by a matter of greater concern. Clearing himself first enables the therapist to make that appraisal.

Disturbances in any participant during the interview, including the therapist, belong to the interview. Should the topic have been the exclusive concern of the therapist, when finished he can announce honestly and invitingly:

> Well, that takes care of one of our problems. Now, I'm ready for another. This time, you suggest one.

The personal responses of the therapist are not restricted to disclosures that would otherwise be harmful to the therapeutic process. Personal responses are also part of the therapist's authentic behavior and are included at will. Impeding personal reactions, usually the ones therapists would prefer to exclude, must be revealed: sharing casual personal reactions is optional.

Casual personal reactions make the therapist a living person and the therapy less artificial. They can also be beneficial for family members. For instance, appreciating the efforts of a youngster, in addition to simply guiding him in his efforts to talk with his parents, can give him a helpful boost. But such commentary must be a personal response and not a matter of professional routine. The integrity of the therapist's participation is the issue.

The following example continues with Tina's parents and demonstrates what is usually the most difficult, yet the most common, personal reaction for therapists to expose: frustration.

As a consequence of her incountering work, Mother's chronic depression begins to disappear. She dresses better, behaves more spiritedly, and is more actively engaged with her family. But the family difficulties were not rooted exclusively in her withdrawal. This could have been guessed from the beginning. Before a child runs away from home, there must be a serious and chronic defect in the family structure. By the same token, when a mother is permitted to languish in a relentless depression for two years, her illness is obviously also a consequence and not only a cause of trouble. A persistently symptomatic family member signals a defective family milieu. Tina's running away was the first *audible* signal but not the first signal in this troubled home.

Mother and Father begin to restore their family. As they discuss various matters, their negotiations frequently break down and needed conversation is abandoned. Now, Mother is the one who tries to discuss things, such as the constant fighting between the kids, while her husband, as at the outset, avoids. The more specific she becomes, the more general he gets: the more intense she becomes, the more indifferent he seems. The therapist has tried every way he knows to break this deadlock: from pointing up his evasiveness each time it occurs, to suggesting to his wife alternative ways to meet him. Nothing works. The therapist's growing exasperation is shared with the husband.

> *Therapist:* Damn it! Nothing helps. Explanations, encouragement, soft words, harsh words. Nothing helps: absolutely nothing. Your wife cries for your cooperation on urgent family matters, and all you can come up with are platitudes and evasions. I don't know what in hell to do with you.
>
> *Husband:* What's wrong with trying to be nice to each other?
>
> *Therapist* (angrily): Because your niceness isn't nice at all. It solves nothing and your family gets chaotic and unhappy. But we've been through all this before and it means nothing to you, apparently.

Specifics are always in order.

> A dozen times, at least, I've told you to stop asking questions and still, you keep asking them. I answer them and you ask the same ones over. If I thought you were stupid, I could forgive you. You're not stupid. You're an evasive idiot. I don't care

114

that you learned that way of behaving before you could know better. It's time you did something about it and you don't even try. You just continue on your absurd, blind way.

The words are for the husband, the affect for the therapist. Since growling is out of style, humans must find words to convey the anger. It's better when the words have a guiding message, but it's best when the words and affect are sent regardless. Shit! Hell! Damn! and other expletives have their value in discharging overkill.

Warning: Keep curses fresh. When used as a matter of routine they become clichés and lose potency.

In the wake of the discharge, the therapist's participation becomes a mixture of cleaning away remaining debris and guidance. Seeking feedback is the first guiding step, if it does not come spontaneously.

> *Therapist:* Now! Say something nice to me!
>
> *Husband* (smiling): What is there to say? You're entitled to your opinion.
>
> *Therapist:* And you're entitled to yours. And, I'd like it.
>
> *Husband:* I do the best I can.
>
> *Therapist:* Everyone does. That's no answer.
>
> *Husband:* What should I tell you: I'll try to do better?
>
> *Therapist:* No. I'm not interested in promises. I'm interested in you: in what's going on inside you right now.

Intense personal participation is not likely to pass without arousing intense reaction. Giving and seeking the intense personal reaction often breaks deadlocking.

> *Husband:* I'm upset, naturally.
>
> *Therapist:* Let's hear about it.

Husband: I always get upset when things get emotional.

Therapist: I'm not interested in always. I'm interested in now.

Husband: Well, right now my stomach is quivering.

Therapist: And, is saying what?

Husband: I'm scared.

Therapist: Go on. What are the details.

Husband: I'm not sure . . . I'm afraid I'll lose something . . . like get wiped out . . . (smiling) reminds me of home.

Therapist: Specifics, please. And without the grin. When, where and with whom? Go to the first picture that comes to mind.

The husband has moved from his evasive behavior towards its underpinnings. The therapist, his equanimity restored, now guides the quivering stomach by teasing out the specifics, refining the message and seeing that it gets delivered to its proper target(s).

The therapist's vigorous disclosure of himself may do more than just relieve him and permit him to guide. It can, as any personal expression, lead to further awareness about himself. For instance, his expressed frustration could bring him to realize an intense life-long exaggerated pressure to be helpful. An older brother syndrome may suddenly flash through him and catapult him into a painful awareness. Then it is appropriate for him to continue to reveal himself; telling about himself to this family or going to the heart of the sadness, perhaps by creating his own incounter on the spot.

The therapist who can treat himself as he treats each member in the family with whom he works, creates the optimal atmosphere. Asking from himself no less than he asks from others is his most powerful invitation to personal growth.

3. GETTING IT TOGETHER: THE PERSONAL GUIDE

Successful guidance is measured by its effectiveness; adequate personal participation is measured by the relief it provides the therapist. Getting them together i.e., effective personal guidance is each therapist's creative activity. First, some thoughts on effective guidance.

EFFECTIVE GUIDANCE

Guidance requires more than a knowledge of principles, timely offered. It requires salesmanship. As offensive as that may sound to the professional-minded therapist, it is best looked at squarely. To have impact the therapist must deliver his well-timed wisdom so that it can be heard. To one he may speak softly, to another reasonably, to yet another, resoundingly. To each, he must speak differently at various times. The therapist strives for the sound that is audible, for the words that stir.

A wife and husband explore their discontents. To the wife's expressed desire for a more personal response, the husband consistently responds more like a travel agent than a husband. He is unerringly friendly and serviceable. Consider these four graded interventions which essentially say the same thing.

1. Simply

> John, your wife wants your personal response, even though it may be negative. Instead, you bring her friendly flowers and serviceable information.

2. Elaborating

> I know you love your wife. She knows it, too. But knowing it isn't enough. She doesn't experience it. Giving her what she asks for and doing what she wants isn't all there is to love. She must have your wishes—though they may oppose hers; your objections—though they may cause her pain. Those are the deeper, more personal expressions of love she asks for when she tells you she doesn't get enough from you. She means *of* you.

3. Directing

> Enough about her desires. John, I want yours. What do you want from her? What does she do that you don't like? She can't be perfect. Tell her what's missing.

4. Provoking

> When in hell are you going to stand up to her with what *you* want instead of taking all that crap from her as though your only desire is to be her favorite toilet?

Selecting the most evocative comment is learned directly from personal experience with the person. If reasonableness leads to passive understanding, it is avoided. If encouragement motivates action, it is offered. If confrontation gets the necessary responsiveness, then confrontation it is.

When one family member responds to a soft message, while another is more responsive to confrontations, the therapist may be accused of favoritism. If the charge is accurate, the therapist admits it, telling, if he wishes, what he likes better about the other family member. If the charge is only a reaction to his different approach to each of them, he simply says, for example,

> She listens when I talk. You don't.

INTEGRATING THE PERSONAL ELEMENT

Comments must relieve a proper measure of personal unrest: not too much, and not too little. Too much relief may cause the therapist to become disinterested in further pursuit when pressure is still needed. Too little relief may contaminate subsequent perspective.

In the various examples, cited above, for delivering essentially the same message, there was no consideration of the therapist's need for relief. In actual practice, the therapist may need a ton of explosive relief while the particular family member may benefit most from an ounce of supportive syrup. Or the opposite, the

118

therapist is feeling mild and yet he knows that to be heard calls for vigorous exhortation.

Sweetening The Pot (Modifying Example 1, above)
Excessive distress in the therapist can be modified by generalizing, preambling, parables, humor, or simply by direct disclosure of the problem. The therapist selects the way that fits his personality, yet carries off the disturbing effect.

> Damn it, John. I know you love your wife, but no woman can live on goodies alone. Most men are a helluva lot nastier than you are to Joan, and the women complain less. Every good woman needs abuse once in awhile. Damn! I wish your father had taught you that. Where in hell was he? Don't answer, I don't really care about him just now.

Then, as the steam is spent, remarks may be added which provide more light and less heat.

Inviting help from the recipient or other family members brings with it the reality that no one is pure therapist or pure patient; and additionally, it can be heartening and instructive to a person who often feels inadequate yet dares not ask for help.

> John, I get so damn frustrated with you. I feel like screaming at you, but I don't want you to sulk silently as you've done before when I unload. You know, it's a real drag to see you unable to really speak out and not to be able to help you unlock your mouth. I don't know what in the hell to do now. Can you help me?

During such a process, the therapist can learn something about himself, which, at its least, gives the family member a living example of how to evolve and, at its best, coincides precisely with the member's own inner distress.

> As I talk to you, John, I realize that I'm angry about my helplessness. I've never thought of that before, but it seems

right. It relieves me to say it. I like you and want to be of benefit to you. I can't stand not being able to bring you what you need. Maybe that's what you feel with Joan, too, sometimes.

Salesmanship does not require deception or sham. The best salesmen believe in their product. The therapist's authenticity is still the supreme ingredient. However, while standing on the solid foundation of his genuineness, there is likely a far greater range of intervention available than commonly used. Most therapist's would do well to exercise this faculty.

Reving Up The Therapist's Engine
From previous experience with Paul, the hard confrontation (Example 4, above), works best. Yet, at this moment, the therapist feels either mellow or frankly disinterested. His best bet is to focus on that aspect of himself in relation to Paul's need.

> You know Paul, I can see that you need your ass kicked again to remind your head to take better care of all that's between those two points, but I don't want to talk to you that way now, and maybe never again, even though you are responsive to it. I'd like you to become a bit more responsive to other ways of living with people. (Then inviting response) Any thoughts about how we can get there?

Adding incentive helps.

> Paul, now that your daughter Peggy is almost an adult she often wants to talk with you and share things with you, but she shies away rather than shout at you to listen. We've talked about that before when we've seen it here.

Getting help from the rest of the family is always a good idea.

> What about it, Peg? Maybe you can say something more to your father about what his hard-headedness does to you.

Getting it together takes more courage than skill. The tendency to cop out, to exclude one or the other aspect of the intervention, is formidable; it is neater and more predictable; but far less forceful and certainly less creative.

4. KEEPING IT TOGETHER: THE WHOLE MESSAGE

Eventually therapists stop looking around for innovations and settle, more or less comfortably, into their own personal style of working. Hopefully, for the benefit of the therapist as well as the families with whom he will work, his style will include some mechanism for continuing his own development, some stimulus to keep him excited about what he does, some challenge to avoid the sluggishness and stagnation that comes to all repetitious activity; in short, a means of meeting people in an ever refreshing and productive way. The whole message may be the instrument.

The value of the spoken word has been amply extolled throughout this volume. Not only does it provide a means for meandering down the path of relatedness but it also establishes a vehicle for expanding one's own awareness. Yet, when the moment is at hand, many find it difficult, if not impossible, to speak with candor. The deterents most frequently mentioned are a fear of hurting the other person and a concern about damaging the relationship. Probably a more cogent reason is the fear of expanding consciousness which often follows on the heels of a difficult and personal disclosure and which, like falling out of bed while asleep, can cause quite a shock—especially when the room in which one awakens turns out to be an unfamiliar one. (See Chapter 3 Section 6.)

But it is unnecessary to concern ourselves excessively about reasons. We can simply begin with the knowledge that, irrespective of the horrendous content of the message and regardless of the seemingly reasonable—though always ominous—explanation for not delivering it, hesitation to speak out reveals one thing for

121

certain: the message is incomplete. A whole message ("saying it like it is") is neither horrible nor hurtful; damaging nor dangerous.

> I hate you and that's all there is to it!

is a good opener for a needed conversation, but it is an incomplete message. If, in fact, that were all there were to it, then it—the hating—would not exist. The fear of saying it like it is, is the fear of saying it *almost* like it is, a sensible fear, indeed.

Following are some almost messages (and their accompanying thoughts of disaster). First, from fear-filled family therapists.

> I think the whole damn family is just plain stupid. (They'd never come back if I told them.)

> This couple ought to break up. They never should have married in the first place. (But I feel as though I were playing God if I ever said it.)

> I don't know what to do. (I'd be an idiot to expect people to work with me if I told that to them. After all, I'm supposed to know.)

> My husband and I have the same problem. (They'd lose confidence in me if I told them.)

> I hate the father in the family. (If I told him, he'd never come back and then where would we be?)

Family members stymie with incomplete messages, too.

> Sometimes I just plain don't love my wife, at all. I even have thoughts of leaving her. (I don't dare tell her. I don't know what would happen. I'm afraid she'd go to pieces.)

> I get so fed up being a mother that I sometimes wish I'd never had kids. (I'd never say that in front of the children. They'd never understand.)

> Sure, I hated my childhood. Doesn't everyone? (Tell my Mother? Never! Why hurt the poor old lady. She did the best she could.)

The Whole Message

Contrary to what most people believe, the problem is not the content of the message but rather the fact that the message is incomplete. Take the thought (and its clinging concern),

> I find you disgusting (but I dare not tell you because I want you to see me as a kindly and impartial therapist).

To say, "I find you disgusting" would be a partial message and might well bring undesirable (and unnecessary) repercussions. The whole message is the apparent message *plus* the hidden hesitation.

> I find you disgusting but I dare not tell you unconditionally because I want you to see me as a kindly and impartial therapist.

This is often enough to initiate a fearsome but certainly not a deadly or damaging conversation. If it is nerve-wracking to start, then the anxiety is a part of the whole message, also.

> My heart is pounding as I say this, but I must tell you

The whole message then consists of the recognized message of discontent, the fear of telling it and the desire to be at least, if not lovable, respectable. Frustration, fear and desire characterize the whole message.

In reality, it is not even the disparaging part of the message that causes trouble. Anyone, regardless of what he may profess, can absorb a negative remark. Ironically, it is the *absence of the unspoken part* that makes the message potentially damaging. Its absence creates uncomfortable mystery as it dehumanizes both parties. It is the also revealed fear and desire that bring the message and the messenger to life. (Politeness is often mistakenly substituted for the personal part, with poor results.) The greatest gift anyone can get, though it be at times unpalatable,

123

is the authentic personal response of another. Somewhere inside, everyone knows that.

Some practical examples

> I think you are stupid (and I'm afraid you will not come back if I told you).

becomes

> I want to continue to work with you all, but I often think you are being stupid and I fear that if I say it, you would refuse to work further with me. When I don't say it I become blocked and do not work well.

Going to the specifics of what leads to the diagnosis of stupidity, and inviting feedback completes the sequence and launches the therapy.

If there is no desire to continue working with the family, the whole message is likely to be a bit longer and more exciting. It may even renew interest.

> I don't want to continue working with you all (but I dare not say it).

becomes

> It is difficult for me to tell you that I no longer want to continue working with your family. I can't even tell you why and I don't want to discuss it. I am embarassed that I cannot tell you this without shaking. I know I must seem terribly unfair refusing to even discuss the matter with you. I'm terribly sorry about that. I wish I could just be matter-of-fact about it and simply arrange a transfer for you without all this ridiculous nervousness. Ecccch! I can't stand myself when I'm like this. There. That feels better. Now, what *must* be changed in order for us to work together is

Sometimes the whole message doesn't help, yet it is helpful.

> I don't know what to do (and I feel like an idiot).

becomes

> I don't know what to do just now and I feel like an idiot
> since you come here expecting me to know. I'm new at family
> therapy and often get a bit lost. But I believe in it. Whew!
> It's sure hard to say this. And, I still don't know what we
> should talk about. The book says to ask. Can you help me?

One person may be reassuring, another may suggest something to work on, while yet another may reveal skepticism towards you. Everyone may be lost together for awhile. All, exciting invitations to find one's next whole message.

Whole messages convey pain, not disdain; whole messages are a desire for resolution, though they may speak of dissolution; whole messages seek relief, not revenge. Anyone can learn to say whole messages: everyone can listen to whole messages. Whole messages inspire conversations. Whole messages create new whole messages.

The Declension Of A Whole Message
Whole messages do not bear repetition: they outgrow themselves. The following exemplifies the evolution of a simple personal intervention—the disclosure of boredom.
Initially, the thought may be uncomfortable, and the whole message may sound something like:

> I feel a bit embarassed as I tell you that I find myself becoming
> a bit bored as I listen to the two of you discuss your problem.
> I'm not interested in what you are talking about, yet I have
> nothing better to offer you (in addition to my boredom). I'm
> sorry.

With repetition, the elaborate embellishment and the embarassment will gradually disappear, and the whole message, standing alone, may be, simply:

> I'm not listening.

125

Eventually, when all the possible variations are expressed and all the available responses harvested, the therapist will become bored with his tour of boredom and begin to look around his immediate environs for something better. Then, he is likely to find some of its specific sources.

> I'm lulled by the way you talk to each other. It's all so flat and uninspired, as though no one really gives a damn about the topic—or, perhaps, one another.

Finally, boredom disappears completely from the therapist's repertoire, leaving only action born of experience.

> This conversation is too flat for me. I suggest we talk about

Journey To The Beginning
The whole message is recommended as a way of life and not merely as a gimmick to be applied here and there when the going gets tough. Used consistently, the whole message, in addition to its value in problematic situations, becomes a powerful force for evolving one's own destiny—though generally not according to one's expectations.

With the whole message as the propellant, two interwoven paths are continually available. The therapist can take the interpersonal road, as demonstrated in the examples above, by adding specifics and asking for feedback. Or, he can pursue his own greater integration by digging further for whole messages about himself. Adhering to the latter path will inevitably lead him to—and repair defects in—his core process of separating and unifying. (See Chapter 3, section 4.)

Example
A frequently discussed dislike for the husband in one family finally blossomed into a therapist's frank and overwhelming disinterest.

126

> I don't even dislike you any more. I just don't care about you.
> As far as I'm concerned, it is senseless for me to bother with
> you, at all.

The portentious postscript is added.

> I find it difficult to say these things to you. It seems like
> unnecessary cruelty though I am not aware of any need to
> hurt you. These are the thoughts that come into my mind and
> they belong to you, though, as I have already said, it is not my
> intention to hurt you.

The postscript is decoded by digging for the underlying desire, and
the whole message becomes,

> I really don't give a damn about you and yet I hesitate to tell
> you because I want to think of myself as a caring person and
> one who doesn't go around hurting people. At least not
> intentionally. But it's difficult to reconcile this image of myself
> with my obvious disinterest in you.

The crossroads: the therapist can take the path of specifics and
feedback (which on previous occasions with this man has been
fruitless), or the therapist can search for the underpinnings of
his disinterest. He opts for the latter.

> *Husband:* It's o.k. You don't touch me with what you say.
>
> *Therapist:* It's more serious for me than that. I want to care.
> And the fact is that I don't even care whether I hurt you or
> not. That's an unbearable thought for me. It's my own selfish
> life I'm concerned about just now. Not yours.
>
> *Husband:* You're making too much of a big deal out of the
> whole thing. You look like you're about to cry.

"Because I want . . ." applied repetitiously as a guiding stimulus
can serve as a useful gimmick for clawing one's way down to the

core—provided one looks for the most *painful* sentences rather than the most logical ones.

> (Because) I want my life to have some meaning. I must have some meaning to bear living in a world so full of pain, misery, mystery and cruelty. I have built up a supply of principles, virtues and moralities to cope with this incomprehensible and unconcerned universe. And those principles are founded on caring. Without that I despair; I have no hope. And the cold truth at this moment is that I don't care one bit about you. And that shatters me. I am now part of that wanton world of cruelty that doesn't care. My morals are a sham, a ruse to save me, not you. (Now, crying so hard that he could hardly speak) Obviously I have never cared. I can't bear it. I can't.
>
> *Husband* (disturbed): You're taking it too hard, Doc. It's perfectly natural not to care. Most people don't give a damn most of the time.

The therapist is lost in his own changing awareness. Although it is the first time that the husband has been touched, the therapist neither hears nor cares about his patient's message of caring. He is consumed with the painful realization of his own *not* caring. His mind rambles around in time, discarding coveted memories, suddenly seeing something in a new way—sometimes painfully, sometimes with relief. The crying comes in mysterious waves. Forgotten scenes from past ages pop in and out. Gradually the waves diminish and there are moments when he becomes aware of the room. Finally, he looks at the husband.

> I want to stop here. I want to see you and your wife at least once more a few days from now. Let's see then what we might want to do together. Perhaps we can continue. At least we can see and say how we feel towards each other then. I know I am supposed to invite your reactions—I'm sure you have some—but I really don't want to hear them just now. I want to be alone. (What actually happen depends, of course, on the reactions of the others, as well.)

128

The therapist's dilemma is beyond the issue of caring. Caring is only the topic. His *concepts about* caring have collided with another inner reality, and he is undergoing a healthy crash reaction. (In a healthy crash reaction there is no residual bitterness, self-recrimination, or accusation—only pain.) The reader, as the husband in this family, may be tempted to interfere. It is unnecessary. Nothing need be said or done. The therapist's mental reorganization is on course and his future "caring" undoubtedly will be better integrated and more sure-footed. He needs only time.

The proof that the personal path for whole messages has been taken the full distance is readily discernable in the impact of the messages—on the sender, of course. Personal whole messages, thoroughly spent, inevitably catapult one into a moment of growth. Such moments are characterized by anguish and bewilderment—a temporary state of insufferable lostness. (Should the lostness become fixed, the person has diverted into a psychological blind alley and must reconsider the accuracy of his reflections.)

Such despair is the threshold of altered consciousness. Here one must wait for the internal processes to assimilate the experience before the next move—the next whole message—can begin. It is a time of meditation; not premeditated but of spontaneous meditation.

With the immediate experience—what one senses, how one feels, what one thinks—as an endless source of nourishment, whole messages open the door for family members and their therapists to the infinite and impelling possibilities for personal growth and asymptomatic relatedness.